THE LEADERSHIP RENAISSANCE

BLENDING THE ART AND SCIENCE OF YOU

Teri Goudie
Dave Heilmann
Jim Hutchinson
Caylen Bufalino

TABLE OF CONTENTS

PROLOGUE

ENDLESS POSSIBILITIES OF A BLUE SKY MIND

No one expects the world to turn upside down when they get out of bed in the morning, but sometimes it just does. It usually seems to happen on days with clear blue skies, and that always paints an indelible image on the day. Why do we always remember that the most challenging and painful days typically happen when the sun is shining?

It may be because we like to hold on to something good when everything else is bad. Or perhaps the contrast of light and dark makes the story more memorable and poignant. Maybe the clear blue skies serve to provide a backdrop of hope, a visual mirror of our ability as humans to pivot and react with courage in life's most challenging moments.

Consider United Airlines Flight 232 from Denver to Chicago on the bright sunny day of July 19, 1989. That flight was the plane that lost all hydraulics in flight and had to make an emergency landing in Sioux City, Iowa. One hundred and twelve passengers died, but 184 survived. Your mind may have just retrieved the image of the plane that seemed to cartwheel on the tarmac, but there are other images that should be remembered.

You need to see the captain, Al Haynes, performing miracles in controlling the plane with experience and true grit. You need to hear his use of humor in the last few seconds before he attempted to land on the runway. You need to listen to the flight attendants who jumped right into their evacuation commands even while hanging upside down in the wreckage. You need to imagine the speed with which first responders from miles around sped down country roads to reach the airport in minutes. And finally, you need to meet a man named Larry Nagin. His voice is one of the reasons we wrote this book.

Larry was a senior vice president at United and served as corporate counsel. He was given the task of speaking to reporters in the first live press conference after the crash. Back then, "pressers" were incredibly challenging because journalists only got one shot to get the answers they needed. There was no Twitter and no Google. More importantly, airlines were not able to release many details in those first few hours because families of the passengers still had not been notified.

To prepare for a press conference like this, there is an incredibly intense discussion of what you know, what you can say legally, and how to handle emotional questions about those who died. Crisis can bring out the best in people, but the wrong tone can ruin a brand in minutes. Millions of people are listening to you, watching your gestures, and hoping the aggressive reporters unveil the true story of what happened.

United quickly prepared a room at O'Hare Airport, using an improvised tarp for privacy. The media clustered together, and Larry rushed in to meet the press. The lights were bright, emotions were at a peak, and the questions were challenging because reporters were getting their own details from people on the ground in Iowa.

Nagin took to the podium, adjusted his glasses, and then something extraordinary happened. He used the word "happy." Yes, he was empathetic and honest and strong, but also very human. When asked about those that made it out of the plane he said, "We are so *happy* there are survivors."

It was then that the tone in the room shifted. It didn't shift because of his messages. The word "happy" would never have gotten approval in a legal review. The tone also didn't shift because he won a battle with the media. It shifted because he was willing to be human—engaging and hopeful. He used a word we didn't think we would hear for a long time. But it was the right word at a moment when the world was watching.

I have used that clip many times over the years with our clients in media training. In fact, I am proud to say that I trained Larry. Many years later he reached out to me with a simple request. He wanted a copy of the press conference.

It seems that he had been diagnosed with terminal lung cancer and he wanted to show the tape to his grandchildren before he died. I was able to get it to him quickly, and thus the legacy of being human in the world of communication is now part of the next generation.

That is what communication is all about. It is not a game of win or lose. It is what connects us and lifts us up, especially when times are bad. It is a tool to help us evolve and learn and grow. It is not just a script for a Teleprompter: It is the script of life. Communication done right stands the test of time and provides an eternal source of courage, vision, and humor. That is why some of the best communication happens in dark times.

Consider Shakespeare.

It is said that Shakespeare wrote some of his finest work during the plague. A time when people were confined to their homes, and businesses stood still. Emerging from the Plague came the Renaissance, a time when everyday people felt empowered to open their minds, share ideas, and accept different viewpoints. They used art and science to share those ideas in a way that has stood the test of time.

Our most treasured art, groundbreaking science, and literature that can still stir the soul, all of these came after one of history's darkest moments. Dare we say it is happening again. Our post-COVID-19 world is a time when we want to feel connected, when the visual reigns supreme, when we need to laugh, and build, and do all of this with creativity, courage, and unity. Leaders have a once-in-a-lifetime opportunity to capture this golden moment. A chance to do things never done before in a way that creates a legacy of impact. A chance to expand and enhance relationships by using both the art and the science of contemporary communication.

The need to add in more art to the science of how you lead was recently confirmed by a Gartner study. It is said that more than 70% of what a manager does today will no longer be necessary by 2024. Artificial intelligence and automation will take over the work formerly done by management. As a result, leaders of the future will have to be more emotive. They will need to inspire and motivate every single day. They will be more like music conductors creating harmony as opposed to bosses using authority as a tool.

Lin-Manuel Miranda knew what he was doing when he created *Hamilton* as a vehicle to capture history through song, strategic lyrics, and dance. He inspired us to challenge our bias and our misunderstanding of others. He stirred our souls in the spirit of renaissance. His amazing work of art on Broadway was one of the many reasons The Headliners was born.

We chose our own Shakespearean moment to write *The Leadership Renaissance* during the time of COVID-19. Building upon a method proven over three decades, it will provide you with the tools and insights needed to have the courage to connect and begin your own new era of impact.

If we did not have the dark, we would not work so hard to find the light. If we did not have strife, we would not have poetry. That is why a young woman named Amanda Gorman was able to touch the hearts and minds of millions of people in six eloquent minutes.

Gorman took to the microphone, at the inauguration of the new president of the United States, to remind us that "even as we grieved, we grew." Wearing bright yellow and dynamic red, she fought her fear of stuttering and delivered a poem for the ages. She said: "We did not feel prepared to be the heirs of such a terrifying hour. But within it we've found the power to author a new chapter. To offer hope and laughter to ourselves."

A renaissance moment indeed.

—*Teri Goudie*

WELCOME TO THE RENAISSANCE

THE NEED FOR ART AND SCIENCE

It was March 2020. Millions of people woke up to what they thought would be yet another typical Monday. They rolled out of bed, put on their slippers, and headed to the kitchen. Normally this would be the start of the two-hour miracle of time management that allows families to work out, eat, dress, board the school bus, and catch the express train to the city.

However, the scenes in this movie had shifted. Possibly for good.

Instead of a workout, people immediately turned on the television to watch death counts. Instead of dressing for work, people threw a clean button-down shirt over a pair of ratty shorts. Instead of handing their kids a lunch box, they handed them an iPad and sent them to the family room for class. The school buses were locked up; the planes had stopped landing; the trains were barely running; and life as we know it had stopped. Not just life, but business as well.

This was a crisis. A crisis so bad that reporters quickly ran out of adjectives. Nothing made sense anymore and everything had to be done a new way, especially in the way we communicate. Zoom quickly became a verb, just like Google. And the change was more than just technology. The change was in tone, and priorities, and visuals. Visuals that allowed people to tame the frightening mystery in their minds and a future they couldn't see.

This change was actually already percolating in a BC (Before COVID-19) world. The crisis just accelerated everything that we had already noted, and taught in our classes, at Goudie Media and The Headliners. The winds had started to shift, but the coronavirus came in like a hurricane and accelerated everything.

The evolution of social media has changed the way we listen and talk to each other. But with the hurricane, now all of a sudden, everything had to be shorter and more relevant. People tuned you out if you didn't hit the "so what, who cares, and what's in it for me?" in your first fifteen seconds. We started to delete emails based on subject lines and hate PowerPoint but love YouTube.

We were all trying to connect in a "world without handshakes." A virtual world where people were being asked to put big ideas in a few well-selected words and then talk to a tiny green lens. A digital world where everyone is a citizen reporter sharing experiences as they happen. An urgent world where when the spotlight gets bright, the story has to be right.

We personally experienced this in our work with the company that delivered the first diagnostic tests for COVID-19. Just weeks after the pandemic started to spread, a group of dedicated scientists and engineers came up with a diagnostic test that could be distributed on a global scale. It was complex technology and what we knew about the virus was changing every day.

Sunday became the new Monday as we were asked to coach our client's scientists to do media via this newfangled thing called Zoom. However, we knew from experience that people tend to be their best self in times of crisis. Our guidance was clear and easy to use: be human, paint verbal pictures to mitigate fear, and enable the American public to ask the right questions about testing. If you know how to ask the right questions, you usually get the best outcomes.

The key for spotlight moments does not just come down to the legally approved messages on a piece of paper. Those messages are vital ingredients but you only create impact when you know how to weave them together. Ironically, you can only move healthcare forward when you know how to connect the molecules and understand the connections within DNA.

Connection is a vital force and that is why The Headliners decided to merge our knowledge and our passion to elevate what people can do with their leadership voice.

You are about to meet four very different people. We look different, we sound different, and we represent a couple of different generations. You will see a little bit of yourself in at least one of us, if not all.

We typically offer The Headliners on a beautiful stage with amazing sound, dramatic lighting, and an audience on the edge of its seat. Well, that's the goal at least.

Today's world is "phygital" meaning a hybrid of physical and digital. Virtual is how we do things so please join us in the theatre of your own imagination. Sit back, pop a cold one, and listen as we teach, laugh and sing our way into your head and into your heart.

ENTER THE HEADLINERS

TRAINING MADE FUN WITH AMUSICATION

In order to speak in a new way, you have to think in a new way. In order to be considered truly innovative, you have to speak in an innovative way. That is the story of the Headliners. We, your authors, have already had our own renaissance moment in our vision, what we teach and how we teach it.

The idea for The Headliners was generated from the desire to have a group of people teaching communication skills in a way that has never been done before. A way to take humor and music and combine that with a proven methodology to uplift people's ability to connect and communicate.

Thus was born an unlikely cast of characters. Teri Goudie, the ABC news journalist turned communication strategist and crisis coach to the Fortune 100. Caylen Bufalino, a social media strategist who started her career in a 30-foot hot dog. Dave Heilmann, a lawyer, humorist, theater founder, and former mayor. (Yes, that's right—a funny lawyer.) And finally, Jim Hutchinson, a *Mad Men* advertising guru and market researcher with amazing musical talent and a wonderful way with words.

Enter "Amusication." Amuse. Music. Education. A brand-new way to teach a proven five-step method that combines strategic communication science with the art of what makes us human.

And why do we teach this way? It is who we are.

TERI: I often wonder how the most shy kid on the playground ended up coaching some of the most powerful leaders in the world. My parents would tell you it was always inside me. I would tell you it took hard work, courage, and a bit of luck.

The luck may have been the high school teacher who read one of my essays and encouraged me to write. Not only did he carve my path as a journalist, but I learned the power of a teacher in the life of a child. I went on to become an ABC News journalist and now, as a communication coach, I get to be a teacher as well. The circle of life.

I met my husband, Chuck Goudie, in the newsroom as he arrived to interview for a job as a reporter at our television station. He claims he took the job at ABC7 Chicago after he saw me in the corner of the studio yelling at a producer. As the story goes, he immediately knew I was the one for him. His destiny. I asked if there was a glow over my head when he saw me because it was one of the most important moments of my life.

I left ABC News when our first child was born and started my own media training company. It was not an easy decision, but it was the right one. I went on to have five children in six years and owning Goudie Media gave me a lot of flexibility, especially when my husband had to leave for weeks at a time to cover wars, hurricanes, and major events like 9/11.

My global consulting firm grew quickly because, early on, I developed a five-step method that clients could trust and use in a practical way for everything from media to presentations to town hall meetings. The method I built was simple, genuine, but very powerful. Clients found new ways to use it every day and we expanded into training for satellite interviews, e-mail, and social media.

Today, with almost three million miles logged in the air, I work with everyone from major CEOs, doctors, lawyers, scientists, farmers, and Olympic gold-medal winners. I get called in for major crisis situations, company mergers, life-changing medical discoveries, product launches, and executive development.

Every day is a new topic to research and explore. That keeps me happy as a journalist. Every day is also a chance to impact someone's life as a teacher. I have learned that no one is ever truly secure when asked to speak, and I thrive on watching people stretch and grow with kind and courageous guidance.

Life begins outside your comfort zone, and so I try to push myself the way I push my clients. Pushing yourself past new boundaries helps you learn things about yourself you never knew. It creates empathy, strength, and understanding that can be used in daily life both at work, and play.

I have jumped out of airplanes, been in the water with great white sharks, driven into funnel clouds, climbed Mount Kilimanjaro, and completed many marathons and triathlons. I once asked my friends to throw a pie in my face when I least expected it. That one was a sheer delight.

When you know what you are capable of, you start to define the story of you. When you know the story of you, you find the confidence to create new stories for the people you have yet to serve.

When you connect to the people you have yet to serve, growth happens.

I believe that the world's best leaders are true masters of hospitality. They know how to open up their hearts and minds, welcome you into their world with the gift of an idea, and then make you want to stay with them. The mission I put before you is this: how can you use communication to create friendships with people you may never meet? That is our calling and potentially the start of your renaissance moment.

CAYLEN: Crossing the graduation stage at The University of Missouri in 2007, I looked out at a sea of black and gold and felt a surge of gratitude to be starting my career on the brink of a communication revolution (thanks, social media). It was the eve of an adventure of a lifetime. Behind the wheel of a 30-foot hot dog. Yes. Hot dog.

It will be my "fun fact" at cocktail parties for the rest of my life, but being a spokesperson for Oscar Mayer, and driving the beloved Wienermobile around the United States, shaped my career and taught me the essence of what communication really is: people connecting with people.

After I had my fill of "bunderful" (I know every hot dog pun out there - good and bad) travel, I turned in my Wienermobile keys and spent ten years at two large public relations firms, collaborating with brands as they navigated this new era of social engagement. I started to notice how we check our phones before our feet hit the floor in the morning. I started to hear my clients talk about bloggers and influencers as their first choice to represent their brand. We started to experience a news cycle that literally never ends. Thanks to Twitter, Instagram, and TikTok, we have changed the way our brains crave information. Everything we say now needs to be three things: simple, visual, and memorable.

I joined Goudie Media in 2014, teaching leaders and consumer advocates in the world of food, technology, and healthcare about how these changes impact the work they do. My goal was then, and is now, to help people recognize the way social media has changed how we communicate both digitally and in everyday communication.

I am also what many call a "Millennial Mom" to two young boys. They knew how to use their fingers on my iPhone before they could talk. My oldest son is already learning how to code in school (he is FIVE!). Both boys have mastered the art of virtual communication, which is a blessing to be able to have an authentic connection with family and friends around the world. My experience as a mom has directly impacted how I teach communication. I am honored to work with clients that are literally shaping a world that will allow my boys to grow and thrive.

So many people today claim to be communication experts. Even today at the University of Missouri, a journalism powerhouse, there are at least four different degrees with the word communication in their title. But I'd be willing to bet very few people could accurately define the difference between each degree. And that's the beauty of it. There is so much room for interpretation that you can use its magic in endless ways.

Communication is the essential universal tool when it comes to connecting people. We need connection more than ever to rebuild communities, re-establish relationships and re-set life to be stronger than ever.

DAVE: Well, I wasn't shy like Teri and I've never driven a hot dog. Not once. I was mentally tortured as a child, however. I had an older brother who would open the window by my bed during the Chicago winters to let snow blow in on my face. He found my screams amusing.

I thought of many intriguing ways to smother him. After all, the most creative ideas are born out of a desire to relieve stressful situations. Perhaps those were the formative moments of learning that stress is most quickly relieved by humor. Although it did take about thirty years to find it funny.

My eyes were opened to humor early in life because of musical theater, specifically, musical comedy. That began at age twelve and never really stopped. Along the way came comedic improv in Chicago, some radio and TV commercials, a degree in broadcast journalism, and years of directing shows and writing original scripts.

I remember being in the musical "Singing in The Rain." I wasn't the glamorous Gene Kelly role and could never dance like that. I played the sidekick, a character named Cosmo Brown, who has this crazy funny song called "Make 'Em Laugh." Each evening, the audience would walk into the theater waiting for the title song and the magical dance in the rain. Then this one would hit them out of left field. The response reflected the truth of the song's lyrics, "don't ya know, all the world wants to laugh."

Indeed we do.

So I had this one side of my life: very fun and active in the arts and communication. Then came the other side—the practice of law—where humor goes to die. Yes, we're the ones who write those 18,000-page HR manuals that everyone hates.

I suppose I could have kept my two worlds apart, but when you work around lawyers every day, there was just so much material. I couldn't resist. It began with annual humorous speeches at firm events and over the years grew to a daily part of my law practice. Why? Because I could see the profound impact humor had as workplace stress was increasing in our country. Whether it was a judge, jury, client, adversary, or coworker, they needed that release. And most of the time, they never saw it coming. Therein lies the strength of humor—the unexpected.

One critical point. When I talk about using humor, I am not referring to telling jokes or "trying to be funny." No. It involves timing, the lens with which we see life's events, and recognizing what others may find humorous. There is both an art and science to it, which I will address in more detail later.

Now because law wasn't argumentative enough for me, I also had fun in politics, including eight years as mayor of one of Illinois' larger municipalities. You'll find this hard to believe, but people actually had complaints. I can tell you that in the thousands of conversations and emails I had with residents, no approach worked as well as humor. It always reduced tension, brought warmth, and instilled confidence.

What I have experienced in my life is gaining validity at a critical time. Right now, organizations everywhere are striving for a positive and inclusive work culture. Humor has a role to play in that new healthy workplace. In fact, science is now adding proof to what we already assumed to be the benefit that humor can bring to our health, to our communication and to our businesses.

Humor is one of the greatest gifts we have been given in our lives and has now become one of the most powerful assets to any organization today.

JIM: How did I end up being what Teri calls a brand guru, music lover, and question master? I guess it all started as a little kid.

There are pictures of me at three years old sitting at a toy piano, banging away. Fast-forward through years of piano, guitar, and choir lessons, and I ended up learning how to belt out a song from Lloyd Tuttle, the most wonderful music instructor on the planet at the time, in my humble opinion of course. He taught me everything including proper stance, breathing, diction, and projecting emotion when I sing.

I also love to act. I've performed in musicals and community theater throughout my life, singing a range of songs from "Grease" to "Les Misérables" to "Hamilton." Performing has always been a form of communication for me, not in a verbal sense, but in a broader communal sense. Singing and acting are my gifts to others. I love creating something and sharing it, particularly when I know I'm singing, for example, a friend's favorite song at a house party. My all-time favorite tune to sing is "Your Song" by Elton John—one I always dedicate to the love of my life, my wife Donna.

But beyond music and performing, I've also been fascinated by the world at large, questioning everything. I ask myself, friends, co-workers, clients, basically everyone about everything.

Early on, this blend of endless curiosity and love of performance led me down the path of journalism. I could study, question, report, and be on stage all at once.

So, I ended up studying speech and communications at the University of Michigan. And right after college, I was hired as a daily street reporter for WTOL TV, the CBS affiliate in Toledo, Ohio. I learned so much there about the importance of diving quickly, but also deeply, into the background of each story. I remember, after just four months on the job, interviewing John Glenn for the Sunday evening news in the year he was running for the U.S. Senate (which he won in a landslide, incidentally). You don't conduct interviews like that without a lot of research and asking questions first.

But interestingly, during this stint in the world of news, I missed the theater stage, music, humor, and art. My dad suggested I might like advertising better, where I could tap my creative spirit by writing commercials, funny bits, even jingles.

So, next thing I knew, I had pivoted into the world of advertising, first at United Artists Productions, and then off to New

York City, for two decades of incredible experience as a senior executive with ad agencies DMB&B and J. Walter Thompson.

And boy, did I learn a lot there. I helped guide the development of advertising for major corporations including Procter & Gamble, Sprint, and Princess Cruises. Along the way, I learned how important it is to truly understand a brand's target customers, their unmet emotional and rational needs, and how best to communicate with them.

This experience also taught me the importance of creating powerful, concise advertising briefs for each brand. Once armed with a great brief, the creative team would then come back with an artistic masterpiece—the script, the cool visuals, the jingles—that would cement each brief into strong advertising stone. I loved the opportunity to work with each team in deciding which options had the strongest chances of success.

Then came one last pivot in my career. I was approached by a world-class market research team, asking if I'd be interested in becoming a market research consultant, a person who asks a myriad of questions. I'd get to travel the world, engage with people of every sort, ask deep, intriguing questions, and help companies understand their audiences better. In short, I would be able to help uncover the initial consumer insight, and then advise my clients on where to go from there. I worked with Fortune 500 companies including AB InBev,

Pfizer, Disney, Merrill Lynch, Marriott, Uber, and United Healthcare.

I've essentially led a life devoted to listening to and understanding people and then creating content—be it strategic background for a brand or the gift of music—to help lift others up. It's been wonderful.

* * *

For The Headliners, communication is all about connecting with people. People seem to forget that in today's world, even when it comes to social media, communication is still all about a person connecting effectively with another person or a group of people. More simply put:

The mission of communication is to create friendships with people you may never meet.

TERI: In a number of ways, the creation of The Headliners was ahead of its time. Even before COVID-19, no one, especially Generation X, wanted to sit through a one-hour PowerPoint presentation. People were getting weary of going to conferences and attending session after session with only a ten-minute break for true networking. We all wanted more of what you get in a TED Talk: humor, stories, and even music.

CAYLEN: Because humor, stories, and music have always been at the heart of human connection.

Last year, TED came knocking on my door. (Well actually TEDx Chicago messaged me on LinkedIn). Regardless, I was asked to speak about the impact thoughtful communication has on how we build community. Every consultant and coach dreams of sharing their ideas in a way that drives impact, so I was honored to get the invite.

My own love for TED Talks began when I needed a mental break from the chaos of two toddlers. I had started to end my day walking the neighborhood and listening to the most random topics. The most compelling TED talks are so engrossing that I often find myself circling around the block because I *literally can't stop listening.* So as I started to write my own speech, I had an "aha" moment. All of those "walk around the block one more time" talks had three things in common. First, the speaker starts with the most important idea they wanted to teach. This is an idea that we will come back to time and time again in the book. It is the cornerstone to what The Headliners teach.

Second, every good presentation has at least three stories or examples from real life. Crisp, visual stories are how a neuroscientist or chemist can keep us on the edge of our seats speaking on topics that the average person would normally find dull and dry. Stories that the audience will see in their everyday life. Finally, every good presentation needs to have an element of lightness or humor. Dave, our humor guru, will dive into this deeper later on in the book.

TERI: Your focus should always start with how to make your communication as compelling as possible. You can do this by letting people know that your mission is to be of service. In the upcoming chapters we will share with you the simple, yet powerful, methodology we teach others to become the best teachers. Teachers know better than most how to grab and hold attention, generate new ideas and insights, and, most importantly, create long-lasting memories that can change lives.

JIM: Every teacher has a curriculum guide, and every movie director has a script. I couldn't sing a new piece of music without a score, and when conducting focus groups, I always had a detailed guide. You always want something that ties it all together to create an experience.

TERI: I always like to remind people that no one memorizes messages when they walk into a dinner party. You would be a pretty odd guest.

DAVE: Like a politician, you might say.

TERI: Right. We want you to have an infrastructure for how you speak. Much like watching your favorite movie.

DAVE: Yes, the one you have seen fifty times but when it pops up on your screen and doesn't cost $4.50 to rent, you can't help but watch it again.

TERI: You know the ending. You know that Maria gets over the mountain with the kids and that ET goes home. Yet, you watch it again and again because the narrative flows and there is an inspirational lesson to be learned.

CAYLEN: I was fine with ET going home because he was super creepy. The point is that you can identify with the characters. You feel the tension of fighting against an enemy. There is also a reason that people resort to movies for first dates or family night. Movies pull us together, take us through the same emotional journey *together.* There is no better bonding moment than jumping out of our skin when Jaws jumps out of the water for the first time or sobbing through the ending scene of *Love Actually.*

JIM: And don't forget about a great musical score. *Jaws* was basically three notes and many of us still hum those three notes when we dip our toe in the ocean.

DAVE: What's interesting about that movie, Jim, is that despite the terrifying story, one of the most memorable lines was a humorous one, when Chief Brody first sees the shark and says, "We're gonna need a bigger boat." Throughout the history of film, writers, directors, and actors have relied upon humor as a necessary component of the story, no matter how dark or serious the subject matter. Hitchcock, for example, believed that suspense only had value if balanced by humor.

TERI: In essence, the best presentation you ever give will be like watching your favorite movie. Every time you watch it, you learn something new about yourself and you find a new path forward. That is why you want to connect all the right elements in the all the right ways. No messages or talking points allowed. We want a river of interest, not a flood of data pushed upon us in our busy lives.

CAYLEN: The key is to all this is actually very simple and that is why our approach is globally known and respected. To be the best you can be, we are about to give you five simple steps. These are the steps Teri has been teaching for over thirty years. They work because they are practical and enable people to speak in a way that is simple, visual, and memorable.

DAVE: Method is something most people trust whether you are a scientist, an engineer, or even a lawyer. And lawyers question everything. But I digress.

Ladies and gentlemen, without further ado, the Headliners present to you: our five-step method.

STEP #1

BE A TEACHER, NOT A TELLER

Moral of the story: How to connect in a world without real handshakes.

TERI: "These are unprecedented times." That is the absolute worst opening line a company can use in communication right now. Everything has become unprecedented, and if you begin your communication with the obvious, you will find yourself adrift in the sea of sameness.

JIM: Which is just a terrible sea to be adrift in.

TERI: It is, because everyone gets sick. Sick of hearing the same opening line. And that opening line is the most important thing we teach. The opening line is a one-sentence predictor of how interesting you will be and how much you really care about your audience. It tells us everything about your mindset and starts the clock on how long we are willing to listen to you.

It signals your intent and intent opens the door to trust. No one wants to hear a "verbal selfie." It is easy to start any conversation or presentation by talking about you and your company.

CAYLEN: Sure, your brain loves when you start with what you know best. It says: "You've got this. You know YOUR story. This is a safe place to be." The reason we love selfies is because it gives us a chance to look in the "mirror" and make sure what everyone else is seeing (hearing) is good enough.

TERI: But the audience is saying: "So what, who cares and what's in it for me?" Their brain is saying: "Same old same old. You can nod off right now or, better yet, check out that text that just popped up on your phone."

DAVE: Even take a call from Scam Likely.

JIM: What you start with usually tells your audience what you care about most. Do you care about the customer, the company, or yourself?

TERI: The best way to find that opening line is to think of yourself as a teacher, not a teller. Start with something that immediately changes the questions the audience is asking about your topic.

CAYLEN: Think of the way tech companies disrupt the market with technology to change the questions we ask about the use of devices. Do the same with the way you speak.

TERI: People follow those who know where they are going.

DAVE: What often pulls your listener away from you is something more entertaining. I'll never forget my soft-spoken philosophy professor droning on about whether a ball can be in two places at one time. And all I thought was, "if that's the problem, get another ball." Anyhow, I chose to watch a disgusting centipede take 13 minutes to get from the front to the back of the classroom because that was more entertaining.

Since attention spans have never been shorter. Take a cue from the most popular teachers. Use humor to deliver the lesson.

CAYLEN: We spend so much time on the "how," but when you tell your story, when you want to connect with people, you have to start with the "why." Because you know what that does? That changes the questions that people are asking. When I am prepping an executive to do a live business show—CNN, Fox, whatever it may be—I teach them to take that first question, and to answer it. You have to answer it. But then start with that most important point that you want to teach.

JIM: We call it the anchor statement. A simple statement that can be simply told. A statement that is all about the audience, not about you. A statement that is bold, surprising, and bound to be tweeted. An opening that positions you as a teacher, not a teller.

TERI: Your intention needs to be the foundation of that statement. We have all seen the scene in a sitcom when the nervous young man rings the doorbell to pick up his date. There is sweat dripping down his face. Inside is a grumpy father who bellows, "Young man what are your intentions with my daughter?"

DAVE: It's not only in sitcoms, Teri. A friend of mine once rang the bell to take out a much younger girl. When the mom answered, the sweat began dripping down his face. He discovered that he had also dated the mom.

TERI: And I'll bet she slammed the door in his face.

DAVE: She did, and he deserved it.

CAYLEN: Just like a door can slam in your face with your listeners when they don't know your true intention. To focus on this, ask yourself: Why am I speaking to this audience? What do I want them to do? What is my true intent? That will help you find your anchor statement.

TERI: I was training the CEO of a major restaurant chain recently, and he had planned to start his communication by saying, you guessed it: *"These are unprecedented times."*

JIM: And then he handed you the check.

TERI: No. But I said to him, "If you Google that line, there are fifty other CEOs using that statement today. Let's focus on your intent. When you are clear in your intent, you open the door to trust."

I asked him what he actually wanted people to do after they watched his interview. He said that he wanted people to feel safe to come back to eat despite COVID. I suggested that people might come back once because of safe procedures, but we are usually loyal to restaurants because of great food and memorable experiences.

Together we found a new anchor statement for him to use: "Safety is the vital first step if we want to help people rediscover the joy of dining out." He got booked on most major networks and his company did very well financially during the COVID crisis. Let's focus on your intent. When you are clear in your intent, you open the door to trust.

CAYLEN: A good anchor statement creates a verbal impression that is a true gift to your audience. People aren't looking for long, lingering lectures anymore. Scripted messages or well-practiced talking points aren't strong enough to engage.

DAVE: And we live in the Engagement Era now. 75% of your effectiveness happens in the first 15 seconds.

JIM: People don't want or remember messages or sound bites. They want an experience with you. They want to know that you are more interested in them than you are in yourself.

TERI: Whenever you communicate, your mission should always be to create long-lasting relationships, oftentimes with people you will never meet in person. Your customers, other patients, the fans who cheer for you every Sunday. Great. How do you do that?

First, begin by seeking to understand the new environment we live in. It's a world where the economy of communication has shifted dramatically. Never before has there been so much information to share; and never before have people had such little time or the physical space to share it.

JIM: And it's what the best communicators bring, whether talking about a brand, explaining a new policy, or speaking at a press conference.

CAYLEN: The goal of the anchor statement is clarity. As we said, it should not be a "selfie," all about you or a long set-up sentence. It must be clean and crisp and enlightening.

DAVE: And grip the audience right from the start. Think about the last action movie you saw. That first 10 to 30 seconds where the car is flying off a bridge, or the hero is swinging from a helicopter? That's the kind of attention you want: people on the edge of their seat, leaning forward, and wanting more.

TERI: Even more importantly, you can use that statement to disrupt the moment and to change the questions people are asking. You can control the direction their thoughts and expectations are headed if you get their attention quickly. They may have walked in thinking one thing, but a disruptive anchor statement is a great way to shift their attention to what's really important.

CAYLEN: That's why your anchor statement should be about the most important idea or concept you want to teach. Define this moment in time.

Connect with your audience by declaring why you do something rather than ***how*** you do it.

TERI: The anchor statement is a declaration about something that effectively connects and anchors your audience to you and anchors you to your audience. Your anchor statement needs to be an idea that changes the way people look at their world. Simple ideas are very attractive. We enjoy that moment of insight. We enjoy feeling we really understand something.

CAYLEN: So you might be wondering what a truly impactful anchor statement looks like. Here is what our clients respond to the most. An anchor statement should be:

Unexpected. Unexpected and yet somehow familiar. Use the language of your audience and think of your opening as a gift they can't wait to receive.

Simple. A simple, significant statement that captures the attention of the listener. Don't try to be impossibly clever or complex. Simple creates strength.

Thought-provoking. You want your audience to say: "I have never thought about it that way before."

TERI: Here are some recent examples of anchor statements from our clients.

Oncology Physician: Immunotherapy cures the incurable through the power of the human body.

FinTech Executive: Easy is the most true innovation. Radical simplification is the way we will use digital to empower people to invest for the better.

Geneticist: Genes are not your destiny, information is how you control your future. Being informed about your inherited health risks can help you make actionable choices to live a longer and healthier life.

Chief Marketing Officer: Fearless is when you push the outer limits of today's reality to find the outer edge of what's possible. In marketing, you start that push at the intersection of storytelling and business.

Network Chef: People should try to cook happy using simple ingredients. The simplest ideas can make for the greatest experiences.

Biotech Medical Director: There is more we can do to transform human health than at any other time in our history with genomics at the center of our story.

Software Strategist: Agility is the new essential business tool because it gives you flexibility, balance and control.

Registered Dietitian: A sustainable future starts with good health because health is the foundation for everything.

Infectious Disease Scientist: Every test answers a new question and every answer gets us one step closer to halting the pandemic.

Logistics Vice President: The best way to create velocity in a company is to reward behavior faster. Pay now, not weeks from now, to create a sense of freedom, flexibility, and fulfillment for all.

Emergency Room Doctor: The brain is a precious organ that deserves the best of care because you only have one of them.

TERI: All of these anchor statements were delivered in spotlight moments. They allowed the leader to completely change the questions they would get. If you don't change the questions, you can't change the outcomes. Scientists were asking very different questions about coronavirus in October than they were in March. That is how we got a vaccine in record time.

JIM: The anchor statement should be disruptive and play a role similar to disruptive technology. The audience should forget everything else around them and say, "I have never thought about it that way before."

DAVE: And when we say ideas have to be "disruptive," we don't mean in the sense they stir up controversy. We mean in the way they show your employees, customers, or audience you've spotted and identified a new trend or problem; and now you're offering a service, product, or solution that goes above and beyond meeting needs or answering questions your audience wasn't even aware of.

CAYLEN: So when it's time to craft your own anchor statement ask yourself these questions:

> What is the most important idea I want to teach?
>
> Am I using the words, and thus the tone, that will motivate my audience to respond?
>
> Is there contrast in my opening that creates a sense of tension? Resolving tension is a classic energy source of any book or movie.

JIM: A good anchor statement also has a sense of rhythm and harmony, like much of what came out of the Renaissance. It is pleasing to the ear and pleasing to the mind. Just like back in the advertising days.

There's so much to learn from that period that's still incredibly relevant today. One of the classic *real* Mad Men, Bill Bernbach, once wrote: "At the heart of an effective creative philosophy is the belief that nothing is so powerful as an insight into human nature, what compulsions drive a man, what instincts dominate his action, even though his language so often can camouflage what really motivates him." While businesses always want to know what drives their customers, their *customers* really want to know what drives *the business.*

CAYLEN: Another brilliant motivator, Simon Sinek, tells us, "People don't buy *what* you do, they buy *why* you do it." By the way, that is an anchor statement. [Drops the mic].

DAVE: Trust. It has never been harder to earn, never been harder to keep, and never been as essential to communication as it is today.

TERI: Trust is how you build and protect reputation. One of the most respected CEOs in healthcare shared a quote with me that I will never forget. It comes from Warren Buffett. "It takes 20 years to build a reputation and five minutes to ruin it. If you think about that, you'll do things differently."

CAYLEN: It's not even five minutes anymore, Mr. Buffett. It's seconds thanks to social media. We can lose it to a vicious tweet or even a fake or malicious post. We all have seen the stories of when a social media manager accidentally tweets to their client's account rather than their personal account. It may have been a mistake, but now two million followers know how you really feel about the Britney Spears documentary (or worse). We all want to work with people we trust, for a company we trust, and be in professional and personal relationships with people that we trust.

JIM: What's ironic is that in seconds a reputation can be destroyed thanks to technology, while on the other hand, that same technology can be used to create trust where none existed before. Think about it: many of us are willing to get in a car with a perfect stranger to get a ride home at night because thousands of others did first. Uber. Not only that, you'll take your family on vacation and stay in the home of someone you'll probably never meet. Airbnb.

TERI: Given the fact that trust is at play, it's incredibly important in today's world that you maintain your trustworthiness by staying authentic, transparent, and humble. This means going beyond speaking simply to convey knowledge. Again, it means communicating as a teacher, not a teller. It reinforces the need to start with the idea you want to teach, not just a message you want to sell.

CAYLEN: As a millennial, I have a sharp sense for what is actually authentic. We don't want brands to tell us what to buy, but we do want them to tell us how we can feel happier, healthier, skinnier, sexier, more confident, fulfilled, outgoing, intriguing, more popular—the list goes on forever. And for Gen Z and younger, it's even more complicated. Because now they are "woke" to the fact that brands are using algorithms to find them *wherever they are.* So for a brand to feel authentic, more than ever they need to find that core idea that will resonate with the people they want to reach most.

Take Dove's new slant on their "Real Beauty" campaign as an example. Dove caused waves when they had a sketch artist draw women based on their own description of their face and body. Then the sketch artist had someone else describe that same person. Dove filmed the reactions of the women when the two portraits were unveiled side by side. Each woman was floored because the image that others saw of them was one of happiness and brightness. Dove actually moved the needle on our core beliefs about ourselves.

Recently, they again transformed our traditional way of thinking about beauty with the "Courage Is Beautiful" campaign, featuring faces of healthcare workers masked by the protective gear they were wearing during the coronavirus crisis. Bravery is authentic. Being bold is authentic.

JIM: Yes, that was a brilliant move. I remember an AdAge interview in which Unilever's brand leader, Alessandro Manfredi, noted, "Conversations about beauty, however relevant they might have seemed a few months ago, now seem superficial."

TERI: When you speak from a pure heart, and set the intention to share what you know to be true, you are opening the door to trust. Your relevant and timely addition to the conversation tells people you are paying attention and paying attention to what they care about most. You are listening to *understand* not to reload a message. Trust.

DAVE: Teri, if I can interrupt with a thought on how humor can help build trust.

Think about when you get on a plane and the flight attendant gives a speech about what to do if the plane crashes. There could not be a more serious matter. The flight attendant begins the speech, casually saying things like "in the event of a water landing," as if it's a rather routine landing option for commercial airliners.

As the speech about how your life could end continues, every head on the plane is down, focused on work or perhaps someone with a hacking cough who should have stayed home. Then suddenly the flight attendant starts using humor.

> *"Smoking is prohibited in the lavatories but is allowed on each of the wings."*
>
> *"For those of you who have not been in an automobile manufactured after 1959, you'll need to fasten your seatbelts."*

What happens when passengers hear this? All heads look up and listen. You weren't expecting this and now you want to see who is saying it. You will continue to listen, hoping that the flight attendant says something else that's funny. Why? Because we love to laugh. More than that, we love to take something we've heard that's funny and share it with our friends.

Humor lets you see the genuine person behind the employee—and that genuineness builds trust. It also creates a connection.

CAYLEN: Dave, I will never look down at my phone again.

DAVE: Lie.

CAYLEN: Yeah, it is. But anyhow, another factor to consider when you craft your communication approach is social media.

Social media has forever changed the way we listen to and evaluate one another. People listen for relevancy. They listen for humor. They also listen for the most important thing first. And if they don't hear it, they stop listening. There's just too much information and "social noise" competing for their attention. But if it does resonate in an authentic way, we share it. We re-tweet it, we tell people about it in the elevator, we forward it in our group chats.

TERI: So that is why you always want to start by putting the most important idea into a few well-selected words. You'll note that we started this chapter with "the moral of the story." A top-down approach to communication, in a social media world, will greatly improve the odds of making sure you get heard and remembered.

CAYLEN: The greatest gift that social media has given us is that it allows us to connect and share experiences with people and places we may never have even known existed.

I saw this every single day when I was behind the wheel of the Oscar Mayer Wienermobile. I met thousands of fellow Americans during my 12-month tour. This was a time when social media was really just starting to take hold. Most people had Facebook and Twitter accounts, but Instagram and TikTok were yet to enter the scene. What amazed me the most though, was that all it took was three things to connect with any person we met—whether it was a young mom on a military base, a national news reporter or a 99-year-old grandma at a Walmart in West Virginia:

> **Images unite us.** Even for people who had no idea what the Wienermobile was, the sight of a giant, colorful hot dog on wheels made them smile. And made even the most introverted visitors curious and connected.
>
> **Everyone likes to be heard**. Everyone likes to be acknowledged. Everyone likes to be asked, "how are you doing today?"
>
> **People love to spread "you won't believe what just happened" stories.** I would watch as people walked away from visiting us, phone in hand, furiously texting, posting, sharing their experience.

JIM: I am turning off my phone and putting my Ring doorbell in the trash.

TERI: Actually, that is the worst thing you could do. The biggest danger with transparency is that sometimes in their quest to avoid saying the wrong thing, people end up saying nothing at all. They lean on messages or talking points written by someone else and approved by a team of great lawyers.

CAYLEN: That approach doesn't work in a world where citizen reporters are standing ready to share their experiences. The best way to manage transparency goes back to the word *standing*. Ask yourself: "What do I stand for?" That is the message you want to share.

TERI: "My name is Teri, and I stand for going outside your comfort zone in how you speak as an inspirational way to touch more lives."

CAYLEN: "My name is Caylen, and I stand for using authentic communication to create community everywhere I go."

JIM: "My name is Jim, and I stand for asking deep questions to truly understand the human experience and build upon those insights."

DAVE: "My name is Dave, and I stand for using humankind's greatest blessing, humor, to its fullest potential, every day, in any situation, for every heart you can touch."

TERI: That simple exercise always creates a breakthrough moment in our live coaching sessions. It allows people to dig deep and express the value that they add to other people's lives.

Do you stand for education? Do you stand for the power of health? Do you stand for technology that we can trust, that's safe to use? Do you stand for family, for justice, for community? What is it you stand for? Identify it within yourself and use it as your North Star.

DAVE: If people know what you stand for, if you harness that part of an authentic voice, they will trust you. They will listen to you. They will hear you. They will believe you. It's not so much about even telling stories. Stories are great, and we could tell stories all day, but it's really more about being a *story maker,* not just a *story teller*. Be the one who creates an experience with your audience that they can go out and share that story with others.

JIM: So when you think about communication and the importance of step number one, consider your end game. This is just you sitting back and saying, "What am I actually trying to achieve? Who am I trying to reach? And as they listen to me, am I targeting that always present, 'So what? Who cares? What's in it for me?'"

DAVE: Your anchor statement is also very similar to the opening line in a great book, or the first line of a great movie that makes you think, "Okay, buckle up. This is going to be interesting."

CAYLEN: You were driving before people even had to buckle up, weren't you, Dave.

DAVE: Smartass millennial.

CAYLEN: By the way, an anchor statement can strengthen any form of communication, not just verbal. Imagine your next slide deck with your anchor statement on the first slide, rather than something generic. Your audience will be captivated before you even begin to speak. Unless you use your anchor statement to open, it will be like trying to buy a book with a blank cover. There is no context of what's about to happen. This is a very common mistake and a simple tweak to create more impact.

TERI: You can practice the art of the anchor statement every day, before every meeting and every email. To come up with some great ideas about your anchor statement, keep asking yourself, "What idea am I going to be leading with?" Know that it's that *idea* that ignites people. That's what makes TED Talks so riveting. They focus on ideas worth sharing.

CAYLEN: It's the *idea* that allows you to speak the language of your audience.

Messages are developed on your side of the conversation, but ideas bridge the gap by giving people something they can add to the conversation.

DAVE: If someone tells me, "Oh you need to listen to that speaker's message," I immediately think I have a problem and I need to change. I probably do. But an idea, an idea means that someone has something new that will make my life even better. Like a mocha, with whip.

JIM: Just think of Apple. Their leaders don't stand on stage at a big tech conference and start with, "We have a new computer." Who would care? So does everyone else. Instead, they always begin with their *why*: the true, overarching purpose. For years, that was simply summarized as thinking differently. They stood for making beautifully designed products that are incredibly easy to use. Hearing that, their audience would always lean in, and only then would Tim Cook introduce the product itself.

TERI: Daily practice of our five steps is essential if you want your new leadership voice to be part of who you are, not just what you do.

CAYLEN: Daily. Because with social media and citizen reporters, you are always "on." It's one of the simple but critical things we consistently teach. And being "on" means *always* having an anchor statement at hand. You always have to be ready to tell your story at a moment's notice. A great example of this concept is a story of one memorable late-night trip home from San Francisco to Chicago.

TERI: I was flying back from the west coast to Chicago on the red-eye. It had been a long day of training, and I was thrilled with the idea of a chardonnay and four hours of time on my laptop. I had the aisle seat. Next to me, a guy in the middle seat. As a diva frequent flyer, I knew I now needed two chardonnays. Maybe three.

DAVE: Can't believe they didn't call you and ask if they could fill that seat. So rude.

TERI: I know. That's the least the airline could do. Well, it turns out that my seatmate was very chatty. Despite my tried-and-true trick of putting the headphones on and turning my body away from him, this guy keeps right on chatting. Internally, I was becoming more than a little annoyed, because I just couldn't get anything done.

He was even looking over my shoulder at my screen and started asking me what I do for a living. Finally, I took a moment to breathe, and thought to myself, "OK. What would Jesus do?" So I turned toward him and with gritted teeth and a sorority girl smile, asked him, "OK, what do you do?"

He replied, "Well, I'm one of the heads of sales for Google."

CAYLEN: The plot thickens.

TERI: Doesn't it always happen when you least expect it? So I slowly turned my body completely toward him, shut down my computer screen, and started to tell him about what I do for a living. This is a true story, and we connected in a way that would not have been possible had I not been ready to make the most of the moment.

JIM: Carpe Diem.

TERI: So true, Jim. Seize the day, capture the moment.

CAYLEN: Did you still get your chardonnays?

TERI: Well it was a cross-country flight.

CAYLEN: When Teri first shared that story with me, it was a reminder that *your* story always starts with the why of you, not just the how of your company. And it extends to your online persona as well. Logically, the people we meet—in real life or virtually—are going to look us up when they have a chance. Teri did, at 30,000 feet with her computer strategically angled away from the middle seat. When it's *you* being searched on LinkedIn or "googled", what will be found? I am sure by this point you know what we are going to recommend: Your anchor statement. It should be in the "about me" section of your LinkedIn. The landing page of your website. The lead sentence in your bio.

TERI: Getting this right can also directly impact lives. We see this every day with our clients, especially those in healthcare.

Way back in the 1980s I was working with a company that had developed what looked like might be the first approved medication for HIV. This was during the horrific early panic days of AIDS. My client had traditionally never talked to the media. But because this science was so important, and they were about to release new data from their clinical trials, they decided for the first time they would talk to The New York Times. I was asked to train and prep their head scientist for his press conference. As a scientist, he was naturally very much into detail and the robust nature of his science.

I coached him with strong advice on how to lead with the anchor statement to provide context for this major development. This was going to be the foundational first interview that all future reporters would draw from for their coverage.

My scientist, being an introvert by nature, was incredibly nervous. I said that I would sit next to him for the interview. So he called The New York Times reporter, put it on speakerphone, and began.

The reporter's first question to him was about this amazing discovery. Instead of leading with the anchor statement that we had developed, he started going down the rabbit hole of detail. So on a piece of paper, I quickly wrote his anchor statement which was, "We're turning the corner on HIV." I held it up to him, and he said to the reporter, "You know, let me stop for a second and give you some perspective. What's really happening here with this latest clinical trial is, it looks like we are turning the corner on HIV."

Sure enough, that was the quote on the front page of The New York Times, and it completely changed global awareness of the importance of the work that his company was doing. A bit of follow-up, his company evolved into my number one client, and they still are to this day.

So again, that key anchor statement was proof positive reinforcement of remembering to be a teacher, not a teller.

CAYLEN: So to summarize step number one, start with your anchor statement to disrupt the moment and change the questions people are asking. Begin all communication with the most important idea you want to teach. Define this moment in time. Put down your foundation of trust.

JIM: Like the Industrial Revolution that came after it, the Renaissance witnessed a passion from people who wanted to mix ideas from different disciplines or industries. Those mixes then became the norm as people of diverse talents intermingled.

TERI: Transformation is a journey. The story you deliver will become the story you create with others. Chapter after exhilarating chapter. Any journey starts with a head nod, a wave of the arm, and a pivot by your guide to the right direction. A strong opening anchor statement is that wave of the hand.

CAYLEN: It tells people you know where you are going, and they should join you. You are opening a path that will help do things you never thought possible. A journey you will never forget.

STEP #2

GIVE YOUR AUDIENCE A REASON TO LISTEN

Moral of the story: People will trust you if they know you trust them.

TERI: People seem to forget that in today's world, even when it comes to social media, life is just about one person connecting with another. Even when speaking to a group, each person wants to feel like you are talking to them, and that you understand their hopes, wants, and desires.

It is critical that you find a way to connect personally and professionally in a way that makes the audience say, "Oh, she is just like me." This essential point of commonality opens up an atmosphere of trust where learning and behavior change can happen.

DAVE: Commonality is sometimes hard to find. For example, tell me all the things you think we have in common with everyone in the world. Truth is, not many. One of the very few is humor.

It is an attribute of the greatest leaders in history, what we love about friends, why we married a spouse or left him for someone else, why videos go viral, the number one entertainment choice, and what lifts us when we're down. We naturally gravitate to humor, which is a foundation for the strongest bond and personal connection. That in turn gives rise to trust.

CAYLEN: That's right, and with voices coming at us from everywhere, you don't know who or what to trust. We live in a time where "subject matter experts" are endless, while at the same time, most of us don't know where to turn to get accurate information. Do we trust the BuzzFeed article that tells you that you have three of the four main symptoms of COVID-19, or do you get on the phone with your doctor? Do we trust our neighbor on the Nextdoor app who said he saw a suspicious car driving around the neighborhood, or do we call the police?

Is our nutrition "guru" friend who claims she has the answer to all your weight loss dreams in the form of an easy-to-follow juicing system (which by the way, she is happy to sell to you) the best person to trust?

The truth is, we often do trust people first. We choose our meals based on the reviews of others on Yelp. When we go to rent a property on Airbnb, it's the reviews that let us know those pictures provided by the owner are more than a few years and a few roach sightings outdated.

Your audience needs specific reference as to who you are, where your information comes from, and what you stand for. The old-fashioned footnote now becomes part of the opening, just after the anchor statement.

TERI: As Marc Benioff, the founder of Salesforce, has taught: Trust has to happen before growth. "What is most important to you? Is it trust or is it growth?" said Benioff. "Because if anything trumps trust, then you are in trouble."

JIM: There was a period of time when companies would, for the most part, only talk about their processes and their products. Their self-serving focus only resulted in raising a wall between their customers and their employees. They weren't making their people the priority they should be. That's changing, but we're still not 100% there yet.

TERI: Let's add to what we learned in step number one. After you deliver your anchor statement, you need to give the kind of credibility that enables people to believe what you just said. You have to give them a reason to listen. That is step number two in how you build your conversation and build your presence.

JIM: Your "why listen" opening grabs attention which is vital in what many call our "attention economy." These days, we're all overwhelmed by the amount of information available on any topic. Yet, our attention span is limited and precious. When you pay attention to one thing, you end up ignoring everything else, which is why it is critical to grab your audience's attention immediately. Your "why" really helps.

CAYLEN: Getting someone's attention provides a lens through which to read the events of the moment.

Distraction is a new currency in the social media world. Scrolling through Instagram is like candy for our stressed, chaotic brains. And I choose candy deliberately because even a child knows that you can't have too much. So often we find ourselves in a meeting or on a Zoom—even playing with our kids—but our attention is somewhere else completely. On the beach with our neighbors on their tenth anniversary trip. In the middle of a political rally in Washington D.C. Getting a contouring tutorial from a Kardashian. Our phones and tablets take us places we have never been, but that means that our attention is up for grabs constantly.

DAVE: Can you believe how many people will actually look down at text messages while you're in the middle of a conversation with them?

TERI: Ahh, but they won't if you're making them laugh.

DAVE: You stole my line.

TERI: Because it's true. Your "why listen" statement has to connect you to the audience in a way that is relevant and timely. I have found that sometimes the most compelling opening to a speech comes from something I heard in the hallway right before going on.

DAVE: I have seen you do this, Teri. It not only impresses the audience, but also demonstrates an ability to creatively improvise.

CAYLEN: It's a demo of how they should be presenting as well.

JIM: I remember you telling the audience, Teri, how you had to switch gears at the last moment because what happened that day was important to their lives and what you were about to teach. Every person in that room was now paying attention.

CAYLEN: Here are some ideas on what you should consider for your "why listen" statement. You could start with the story of you, told in three parts: Where you have been (and the results you created), where you are now, and where you are going next.

JIM: Or it could be the research you did before the interview or presentation. Remember our five steps apply to every type of communication opportunity.

TERI: Perhaps you commissioned a survey, perhaps you did a road trip to listen to employees, or maybe last night you read emails from customers. Let the audience know you are listening.

Step #2 is about connecting with people and showing them why they should listen to you. Our faith in humanity is strongest when we are connected to humans. Whether it's online or offline, the best place to connect is in community. Community gives us a safe space where everyone commits to a certain set of agreements. That safe space gives us a chance to experience what we need to experience. If we aim to listen to others, they will be more willing to listen to us.

CAYLEN: We have seen proof of this even during the most challenging of press conferences.

DAVE: Jim, you have done many focus groups with consumers. Doing a press conference can sometimes feel like one big focus group. How do you command attention in those sessions to open up the kind of discussion that enables brands to move in the right direction?

JIM: Interestingly, a focus group is the inverse of a press conference. In a focus group, I would often be asking questions to eight people, while in a news conference, eight reporters are asking questions to one.

That said, there are many commonalities. In both cases, trust is absolutely critical. My groups needed to trust me. And the way I'd get there would start with my "why." I'd introduce our topic, then quickly explain my background and why I was so interested in the topic at hand. Then, before asking a single question, I'd help them let down their guard by:

> **Emphasizing there are truly no wrong answers**, just authentic ones, expressing how they really feel.
>
> **Asking them not to think too hard**. That always got a relaxed chuckle; some had come in wondering if they would "pass the test." I didn't want them to overthink things, just to tell me what came to mind first.
>
> **And finally, encouraging them to be selfish** (which always got a full laugh), after which I'd elaborate: I wanted to know what each of them believed her*self*, personally. Just because one disagreed with the other seven, I definitely wanted to hear everyone's reactions.

It worked every time.

Over the years, I thoroughly enjoyed and honored my chance to understand each person I interviewed; to capture their joys, delights, challenges, and sorrows. I enjoyed the intimacy of each conversation.

Beyond focus groups, I would often conduct lengthy one-on-one interviews, carefully unraveling each respondent's true feelings and beliefs.

Perhaps the most powerful example of the importance of listening came during a study involving a pharmaceutical product and its potential impact on one's life. I was speaking for over an hour with a thirty-eight-year-old man who was using the product. We talked about his background, his feelings about taking the product, how it affected his personal life, and his emotional response to it.

At one point, I asked, "Has your use of the product affected your daily life in any way?" He provided a brief response and then went silent. But his body language suggested he had more to say. I waited. (One of my best questions would often be no question at all, just an earnest look into my respondent's eyes).

Then, all at once he said, "I've never told anyone this before, beyond my love interests, but I'm gay. And that affects my feelings about everything we're discussing."

"Never told anyone?" I asked.

"No. But I feel comfortable in this environment and appreciate your willingness to listen." Our conversation continued in a very positive manner, leading to bona fide, useful, productive insights.

CAYLEN: So maybe that was a "reverse why listen." Instead of you telling him why he should listen to *you*, you made him feel more comfortable by asking why you should listen to *him*. Human-to-human connection.

The idea here is to make your communication as compelling as possible to let people know that your mission is to be of service. When Teri and I introduce ourselves to new clients, we do so with a purpose. Instead of listing out our resumes, we strategically choose past client experiences that would help us connect to those in the room. We always weave in our anchor statements in an authentic way and then bridge to examples of client work that will instantly connect to the people in the room. I don't share my Wienermobile experience with clients who live outside the U.S., but I do mention using communication to connect during my time living in London. We make sure to let doctors know we work with the entire health ecosystem—from payers to hospital systems to medical associations. And we always use timely examples from that day's headlines to both support what we are teaching but also to show (not tell) that we are hyper aware how the news cycle impacts communication.

TERI: For example, let's say your company developed a new continuous glucose monitor for diabetes. One of our clients did just that and now millions of people, including kids, no longer have to prick their finger ten times a day to check their blood sugar.

CAYLEN: Even though our client may never meet all the people who benefit from what they built, they have connected with them via a product that is enhancing their lives.

TERI: Friendships endure and when you think of your customers that way, it can motivate your people.

JIM: Why should people listen to you? Because they trust you. Who are the characters in your story? Hopefully, characters your audience knows, likes, or trusts.

TERI: This story traces back to GE Healthcare which was getting ready to launch a brand-new imaging machine at a major medical conference. It was a pivotal moment in one of the first media trainings I did for this global giant.

We were in a conference room for the training and they were laser-focused on talking about the bits and the bytes, the technology and engineering.

I listened to them discuss this product for an hour. One of the engineers turned to me and said, "What do you think, Teri?"

I said, "It's interesting, but I haven't heard you use the word 'patient' once." And he said, "Patient? Patient? That's not our customer."

"No," I said, "it really *is* your customer." Fortunately, he listened and wanted to know more.

CAYLEN: Everyone in that room learned to use a new perspective. Never forget that the person who will ultimately benefit most from what you do is often not in the room when you are speaking or talking to the media.

TERI: Exactly. You have to visualize that the person you have *yet* to serve is always sitting in front of you. What do they care about? What do they need? What will surprise and delight them?

CAYLEN: After that meeting, one of the company leaders began referring to Teri's method as the "Six Sigma of communication," which was quite a statement since it was the business strategy embraced by GE legend Jack Welch.

TERI: Here are a few recent real life examples of what our clients delivered after their anchor statement. Their "why listen" connection to the audience.

> **Plant Manager After Explosion:** I just personally walked the entire building with the fire chief to make sure all of our employees got out safe. I am so happy to report they did thanks to the extensive practice drills our people perform during the year.
>
> **Global Restaurant CEO:** Over 90% of our system is owner operators. We have to respect what they need to run their local small businesses. This is like having 5,000 CEOs with their own companies and different market challenges.
>
> **Ed Tech CEO:** In today's world of education, there are more questions than ever before and not enough answers. The average classroom has four walls and one teacher. What if we could break down those walls and allow the teacher and students to pose their questions to millions of other people just like them?

Breast Cancer Surgeon: I decided to become a doctor when I was a young girl and watched my grandmother die of breast cancer. That became my mission and today I am proud to tell you that I have treated hundreds of grandmothers and many women of all ages, even the new mothers.

COVID-19 Scientist: We have been working fifteen-hour days to develop our rapid diagnostic test, but I never realized how important it is until I got diagnosed with COVID at work one day. I was able to head home fast and quarantine which prevented my family from getting the virus.

FinTech Subject Matter Expert: Thousands of people from all across America are coming to us every day looking for ways they can benefit from technology in their finances. I can relate to them, because I grew up on a farm and Wall Street seemed miles away from my world.

Pharmacist: I have seen an incredible evolution in cancer treatments for patients. When I was in school, cancer treatments usually happened in the hospital and involved surgery and infusion. Now, just ten years later, we have oral treatments available and patients are no longer tethered to the hospital.

Dean of Major University: I was the first in my family to go to college so I can understand parents' concern about the cost of education rising student debt. That is why we spent three days at the capital meeting with every legislator from every district on what we can do to help our students.

JIM: Often the customer is actually the *customer's* customer. Don't just stop with the company. Consider who their customers are and how they can build trust and connect with them.

TERI: That position became the turning point for GE in the way that they told their story. From then on, they made sure that they were using communication in a properly directed way. Every "why listen" referred to the doctors and patients they worked with to develop the latest technology.

CAYLEN: They always made you imagine the patient was at the design table. They started to use more patient-centered research and thus they garnered more mainstream media attention.

TERI: The media will always lean toward what you are hearing on the front line because that is how they attract readers and viewers. The media will always need you more than you need them if you know how to harness and express the desires of the ultimate audience.

CAYLEN: Your audience may be the people who buy shares in your company yet never meet the CEO. That's your perspective. So in a people-first world, it was really a turning point in the mind of this very powerful CEO. He "got it" that the most important person in their world, the patient, was in the room for that launch.

TERI: Here is how that played out for a biotech company that developed the first FDA-approved immunotherapy for cancer. First of all, immunotherapy means that you're helping a patient's body fight their own cancer. For a cancer patient who feels like they've lost control, such a treatment is powerful on so many levels.

CAYLEN: The treatment is revolutionary, but unfortunately it's also expensive—about $93,000 per treatment. But what we did was recommend that the CEO, who was also a physician, harness the words of the patients and the voice of their doctors. They wanted to be able to get this new drug. For a stage four patient with prostate cancer, this immunotherapy meant hope.

TERI: We coached the CEO and his scientific team. They took their story to the oncologist, the patient advocacy groups, the major medical conferences and the media. Thus, when it was time to consider Medicare and Medicaid pricing, patients and doctors showed up on the front steps of Washington to rally for the medication. They stood up for the value of what that drug meant to them.

DAVE: It means everything. I've sat in that oncologist's office and asked about immunotherapy. Those questions, the answers, and options like immunotherapy, are all that matters.

The innovative minds that bring cures to the incurable and answers to the unsolvable, need only turn to the people who will be impacted most by the discovery to find the compelling story.

CAYLEN: Every day, for years, we had worked with our clients in person, just a few feet away, to develop the finest in communication skills and messaging. Then, in March 2020, everything stopped. What do you do now? You accept the new circumstances, the challenge, and you innovate. You pivot and lead.

TERI: Our clients needed us more than ever, and we knew that virtual training would serve them best.

First, we had to remind ourselves that, even virtually, communication is still people connecting with people. There might be fancy apps and masterminds in Silicon Valley thinking of new ways to label it, but essentially all things social require humans connecting with humans—showing them you have something in common, and why they should listen. Remember the "What's in it for me?" discussion earlier? Still relevant.

CAYLEN: This became so clear with the overnight necessity of virtual meeting apps like Zoom and Microsoft Teams. Mixed in with the requirement for masks and social distancing came a new business tool that work-from-homers couldn't function without. Why? Because meetings result in momentum. They recharge our batteries and give us a roadmap for work.

DAVE: And we want to see someone's face in real time as they "ideate." (Such a good word, isn't it?)

CAYLEN: Great word. When I first *ideated* that I should spend an entire year traveling around in an Oscar Mayer Wienermobile, the thought of their daughter driving a giant hot dog gave my parents pause. But they knew this was much more than helping a meat company sell hot dogs. Oscar Mayer is a beloved brand and a part of the fabric of so many people's childhood memories. The human touch, through branding, would be invaluable.

Indeed it was.

We had countless people come up to the Wienermobile with their kids or grandkids—in more than thirty states—and literally wax poetic about the time THEIR own parents or grandparents took them to see it for the first time. How just the sight of it made them smile. And then they would ask us questions, (usually the same questions over and over again) and I would dish out the same pun-filled answers.

> **Public:** "Do you sleep in the back of that thing?"
>
> **Me:** "Nope! It's not a weenie-bago!"

But I didn't mind. Because I was simply a human, connecting with another human, bringing a smile to their face and a memory that would last a whole lot longer. We had a connection, something in common: my Wienermobile and the love of it.

DAVE: How it made them smile. We can't underestimate that. A hot dog isn't funny (unless someone sits on it. Happened in 5th grade to our nun.) A giant hot dog on wheels? How do you not smile when you walk up to that? An immediate bond through the use of humor.

TERI: It doesn't take a lot to connect. It can be a car, a club, being a mother or a millennial. It can be virtual on a Zoom call with one hundred people or a quick conversation at the Starbucks drive-through. Think about the things that can connect you with your audience. What matters to them and why?

JIM: I agree, Teri. If your audience gets the feeling you understand them, they're much more likely to trust you. And it doesn't take much effort to make it clear you get it. In fact, the best advertisers—after digging deeply to understand their target customers—often capture that insight in just a few words.

A few years back, I worked with a major brand to identify a slogan that—in *two words*—helped potential customers recognize that the brand truly *understood* them. It meant changing the question people were asking in an intriguing way.

The brand? Advil. The simple two-word phrase: "What pain?" Once identified, the team created multiple commercial options, then tested them, resulting in a spot used for the Super Bowl (2017), and winning a gold award from The Advertising Research Foundation (ARF). Their slogan defined a moment in time.

TERI: How did they appeal to so many? What was their important idea?

DAVE: That your head stops hurting like hell if you take two. Maybe three.

JIM: Not quite, Dave. And hey, read the label—two max!

But Teri, to answer your question, the incredible people on the Advil brand really explored the thoughts, habits, and emotions of their consumers, getting a clearer picture of how pain affected their conceptions and self-identify. This process involved a great deal of market research including one-on-one interviews, focus groups, ethnographies, and quantitative research among those suffering from the pains Advil can successfully address.

What did they learn? Sufferers wanted something aspirational. They wanted to put their pain in the rearview mirror. They wanted it to be a distant memory so they could move on with their lives. They wanted to truly *believe* their pain reliever is made by a company that *understands* their pain and how deeply they want to be able to ignore it.

They shared these insights with their strategic and creative teams, who then brainstormed new slogan ideas. More qualitative research followed, winnowing down several strong candidates, but zeroing in on the one idea that truly resonated: "What pain?" One woman said simply, "This is what I want to be...pain-free, strong, and independent." Another said it meant he could "live in the moment, with pain no longer a thought." And one more: "You'll be able to cruise through life...no speed bumps."

DAVE: Sounds like a bunch of whiners.

JIM: They may have been, but the company didn't have a product for that.

But with the "What Pain?" idea, they developed advertising options and explored each among the target audience. In the final ARF research summary, the team noted that, "The big breakthrough moment came when consumers smiled, laughed at this execution, and told us the insight and relevant brand benefit was pithy, memorable, telepathic, and exactly the sentiment they want to exude to their social circle (*defiance toward pain*)."

In short, the brand truly *understood* the audience and captured the spirit brilliantly. They went on to say, "To date, it is the only Advil TV spot to deliver on ALL the necessary measures needed to drive an emotional connection with viewers (branding, enjoyment, engagement, brand appeal, relevance)."

TERI: This extensive process shows how important it is to truly understand your audience. Sometimes, I think about classic advertising campaigns, and marvel at their simplicity and depth at the same time.

JIM: For example, imagine if a national athletic brand had used the phrase "Never Give Up!" What would that suggest they know about me? Well, I guess they think I see myself as a failure, just about to quit. But fortunately, instead, Nike followed its ad agency's recommendation to say, "Just Do It." And when I hear that, I say to myself, now *that* is a company that knows me. They know I believe I *can* win. I just need encouragement, support, and inspiration. And they'll help. Why? Because they really understand me.

CAYLEN: And may I interject that there is no better phrase when asking your husband to do work around the house.

JIM: Here's another hypothetical: What if an insurance company had come out with a slogan that said, "State Farm Insurance. We're #1!" What would that suggest they know about me? Absolutely nothing. In my view, I'd just be one person in a thousand or million. All they care about is themselves. *Why* should I care or listen further? Fortunately, instead, they said (and sang), "Like a good neighbor, State Farm is there." *That's* what I desperately seek when something bad has happened. That's a company that understands what I really, deeply want and need. It's not about them. It's about me.

CAYLEN: Because, after all, what makes a great neighborhood? Shared values, mutual trust, integrity, support, and people who help you recover from the unexpected. (And a TRULY good neighbor knows when to fire up the Margarita machine at the summer block party).

TERI: And also to bring over the Advil.

A good coach always sees something in you that you couldn't see by yourself. Often, that is the best version of you. When you dig deep to connect to an audience, you often learn you have more in common than you think.

JIM: And if you don't know what that is, be a Don Draper and roll in that IBM mainframe to do the research and analytics.

CAYLEN: Use your social media as a two-way street to better understand who it is that wants to be a part of your world. What do they really care about?

TERI: Speaking from "the outside in" is a discipline and a healthy habit for all leaders. Figuring out your "why listen" will give you a way to renew and refresh your point of view every single day. It is a flexible step in the method designed to help you also stay in the right lane of relevancy.

DAVE: Every audience will feel you are talking only to them. The people in your morning meeting will feel as loved as your shareholders who watch you later that night on the evening news. You should rethink your "why listen" for every speaking opportunity on your Outlook calendar.

CAYLEN: If you are doing a podcast, you have to be both entertaining and informative or the listener will move on to someone else that is. If you are doing radio, these days you are catching people in their cars, commuting or carpooling. If you are at a global conference, you adjust every time you hear a different language in your company's booth.

TERI: The key is to establish your point of view in a way that will deliver growth, loyalty, and the always fascinating tale of the human heart.

STEP #3

USE THE DISRUPTIVE FORCE OF UNMET NEEDS

Moral of the story: How to change outcomes by changing the questions.

TERI: To predict the future, you must create it. And in the age of engagement, this is about becoming a story maker and not just a story teller.

In any good story, or movie, you unite the audience by defining what you are fighting against, or perhaps fighting for. What dragon needs to be slayed if you want to save the princess or prince? Who is the mean coach that needs conversion before the down-on-its-luck team can win the game? What obstacles stand in your way if you want to bring down a killer shark on the Fourth of July?

We call this your "dilemma statement," and it comes after the "anchor" and the "why listen." The dilemma statement sets up the unmet need that stands in the way of growth, success, and happiness. The way you define the need directly impacts the odds that people will love your solution.

CAYLEN: Remember that 80% of decisions are made in a time of conflict.

DAVE: Albert Einstein once said: "No problem can ever be solved by looking at it from the same level of consciousness that created it." In other words, the only time we transcend a problem is when we get new fresh thinking about it.

TERI: Fresh is important because the unmet needs in business today seem to reinvent faster than we can keep up.

CAYLEN: The needs of customers are more like those huge windmills you see in wide open spaces around the world. Your challenge is to stop the wind, define it, and then harness the energy. Tension can be a motivator, not just something that hurts.

TERI: First of all, like in the movies, try to surprise and delight your audience by beginning with positivity. Start with the good news, the opportunity at hand. Define this moment in time and then objectively define the challenge, or the problem, in a unique way.

JIM: Cue Mayor Dave and the stop sign story.

DAVE: A man came up to me and, in rather abrupt tones, said, "Mayor, you gotta figure out a way to get people to stop at stop signs. No one is stopping, and you have to do something about it!"

I wanted to say that I thought the signs were pretty self-explanatory. But it's politics, so you have to be nice. So I wrote up about twenty-five humorous sayings like "In the Naaame of Love" and "Whoa, whoa, wait a minute," had these put on red octagon signs, and placed these under the stop signs.

Drivers stopped.

Across the country the press picked up the story, and so did six other countries. Something that simple.

I was asked to do an interview with the BBC, and the reporter said, "Yes, I've read the list of sayings you put under the stop signs, but quite honestly, I don't know that any of them are fahhhny."

To which I responded, "And now you know why we left your country 250 years ago."

The point is that humor made people stop and get the message.

TERI: You got people to think about the problem in a new way. Very creative. Sorry you didn't get a laugh out of the BBC. My clients have struggled with that for years.

CAYLEN: From the very beginning of the COVID crisis we were asked to assist companies that were working on diagnostic tests and treatments. Because it was such a fiercely competitive field, the companies that were able to lead in the marketplace first were the ones that became a target for criticism. And it became very important for us to help them remind people, and legislators, that they were not the enemy. The virus was the enemy.

TERI: We recommended that the scientists explain the way the virus mutates in a very visual way. Those images of the sphere, with red spikes, thus became fodder for tee shirts and Instagram posts. The coronavirus' spiky ball was easily recognized by all and ended up becoming an important visual cue about public health.

CAYLEN: Explaining the unmet need, almost with a mental whiteboard, really helped people see and respect that the virus was the enemy. It was the monster in the movie that suddenly comes into the frame. Everyone wants to fight against it *together,* because now you could see it.

JIM: This is especially important when you are responding to a crisis. Teri, I remember how you helped the CEO when he was asked to respond to the missing aircraft Malaysia 370.

TERI: That is a strong example on how to make sure your people aren't getting blamed in the rush for answers during a fast-moving crisis.

DAVE: This is also a story that reminds us to never be afraid to be human.

CAYLEN: The missing Malaysia Airlines Flight 370 is both a prime example of a negative event where officials led with positivity, and of how they defined a dilemma in a way that people could go out and tell the story for us.

TERI: You may recall that Malaysia 370 took off from Kuala Lumpur International Airport and then disappeared in flight over the South China Sea. No one had any idea what went wrong, and the search area was vast. We were hired to work with the Boston-based company that was chosen by the U.S. Navy to provide a search robot for the rescue operation.

CAYLEN: This was a big moment for the company, and we had just a few hours to prepare the CEO to talk to the media. News trucks were already set up in their parking lot.

TERI: He was an engineer by training and had very little media experience. There was a lot on the line for his company because in reality they were not going to find the missing 777 aircraft. The search was too daunting. He was worried about the long-term impact on his brand and his company's reputation.

CAYLEN: When we met him in a conference room, he had brought piles of papers and file folders full of data. We knew that was not the answer.

TERI: He needed to pull the public into his mission by clearly explaining the unmet need in a way everyone could understand. Just like with the coronavirus, when you understand the problem from your own perspective, you start to feel ownership for the solution.

DAVE: They needed to come up with analogies or comparisons that could be used to reach the American public about this situation.

CAYLEN: Using Teri's method, we came up with a very specific way to describe the unmet need: "We will be searching an area the size of Texas, it is pitch black down there and the pressure at that depth is like putting a Cadillac Escalade on your thumbnail."

TERI: He had his other engineers come in to make sure it was an accurate description, and it was. Out he went to meet the media. Sure enough, every media outlet used that quote. In fact, it was picked up around the world and to this day people remember it.

CAYLEN: He was able to describe his challenge in a way that everyone could understand and relate to.

TERI: Unfortunately, they never did find the wreckage, but his reputation today is as strong as it has ever been. His company was not blamed for failure to complete the mission. The enemy became the vast and complex nature of the South China Sea.

JIM: The story can always go two ways. It could be a classic us-versus-them blame game or something that speaks more to external forces. The way you define the unmet need will determine the path you must take.

DAVE: Again, just like in a film or a good book, use the problem to inspire people to find a solution. The right set-up allows you to say: "Okay now, here's how we're going to solve it together. Here are the amazing results that we can create."

CAYLEN: It is also important to set up the unmet need with verbal pictures. Make sure you create visuals that linger in the mind. My generation is the visual generation, and we are only the beginning. My little boys are learning on iPads, not from a textbook. So the more visual you are, the more memorable you become. In fact, our brain seeks information that is highly visual, simple, and memorable. Think of your favorite GIF, Super Bowl commercial, or cocktail party joke. I bet they share those three characteristics.

TERI: If people carry the pictures of unmet need in their mind, they will remember it when they see visual markers in everyday life. If you define a problem consumers are having with your food product in their kitchens, even your CIO might think about that when he stops at the grocery store that night. If you define the unmet need with pictures about energy shortages, your audience will probably be more likely to turn down the thermostat at home.

JIM: OK, so we've been talking about a brand understanding its consumers. But let's switch gears and talk about a critical audience for every leader: namely, their employees or team members. If you are leading a team, no matter what size, the road to success begins with questions to truly understand who is on your team.

DAVE: Not just giving orders. The right questions lead to improved productivity, innovation, engagement, empowerment, and inclusiveness.

JIM: Far too many managers avoid asking tough questions, particularly ones they should be asking their employees. In a classic study, Sidney Yoshida summed up why employee input is essential: "Only 4% of an organization's front-line problems are known by top management, 9% are known by middle management, 74% by supervisors, and 100% by employees."

Bottom line? Your employees know about the problems you face. Sure, they see the positives, but more importantly, they see the negatives and the opportunities. Unfortunately, if you don't ask for their input, they won't tell you. And your whole team may miss the boat to success.

TERI: How do you avoid that problem? By asking the right questions, to the right groups, in the right way.

CAYLEN: Once you've made the commitment to focus on asking questions, a new world opens up to you and your team.

While it sounds easy, the art of asking questions deserves study. Luckily, Professor Hutch is in the house.

JIM: Here's a game plan:

> **Ask the right questions.** What's your true objective? No matter how big or small your query, prepare your questions in advance. Are you exploring how to improve employee productivity? Reasons for a recent product failure? Unmet needs among customers? Each objective leads to a very specific approach.
>
> **Ask the right people.** Who has the most relevant direct experience with the issue? Don't just ask your peers or assume the internet will have the answer. Ask the team members who are on the front line with direct access to your customers, vendors, equipment, software, whatever's key. Ask the ones who really know what's up.
>
> **Ask in the right way.** Once the first two points have been nailed down, it's important that questions are asked properly. Again, this requires study. But for example, avoid "yes" or "no" questions. Be non-judgmental. Avoid leading questions. Seek true input. Begin with general questions, followed by more specifics. And of course, ask "why?" not just "what?"

CAYLEN: Jim, I have a sneaking suspicion you'll explain more about asking questions in the right way at some point.

DAVE: He always does, Caylen. He always does.

But before we go there, I'd like to share another way to address a dilemma. Let's not forget that a dilemma by definition is a negative. There is a problem. It needs to be solved. And a few phrases Teri discussed earlier bear repeating because they capture so well how the very words you choose—instead of laying blame or complaining—move the negative to a positive:

"Engagement"

"Unite the audience"

"Solve in an intriguing way"

"People will love your solution"

Come to think of it, it's the opposite of politics.

There will be times when you can define the dilemma through a humorous personal story of how that problem affected you. Most likely others had the same experience.

One story I can share is when I was in a lengthy debate one evening with an opposing lawyer who was not getting what he wanted after months of intense negotiations on a contract. Now my belief is that attorneys, regardless of any disagreement, should keep communications professional and civil. Take the work, not yourself, seriously. But this attorney was getting hotter and hotter, and at the end of an hour of this he blurted out, "You just listen to me, DAVE." (When someone is angry, they start using your name with emphasis.) "I want you to know that I've been doing this 28 years, and I don't lose; I NEVER LOSE!"

Very professional.

I responded with the first thing that came to my head.

Well, Tony, I've been doing this 29 years, and I never win. So I'm waaaaaayy overdue."

Silence.

Not the comment he was expecting. After a long pause he started laughing and said, "Okay, okay, you got me." We then talked for another half hour and it was more productive than the four prior months.

The obstacle to negotiating the contract obviously wasn't only about the terms each side wanted. There was more to it for that other lawyer. He saw getting those terms as a personal victory over me, an adversary. The humor, though, reduced that conflict and the "win" wasn't as important.

JIM: Ah, lawyers. You're always so funny.

Now, "the dilemma" also resonates in my years in advertising, given its critical role in every creative brief—the concise summary of a project to inspire a creative team. That's where every great ad begins.

First, each brief starts with the dilemma, often referred to as the consumer insight. What's the unmet need out there? Second, the solution. What does our product or service uniquely offer? And third, why should anyone believe us? What simple yet credible proof point can we include in our message? Nail all that, and you've got a solid brief.

As one example of a great ad brief, NiQuitin (known as NicoDerm in the U.S.) identified the real dilemma among smokers: a feeling that cigarettes have taken over their lives, and that people need to feel empowered to quit. The promise: NiQuitin empowers life without smoking and will always be by your side. Why believe them? The brand doubles your chances of quitting.

Incidentally, one of the critical components of any strong communication is to create a thoroughly unique statement. You definitely don't want to sound like everybody else. If you offer up the same cookie-cutter statements everyone else is using, you will lose the opportunity to create that special, unique experience around what your company does offer.

DAVE: Besides "unprecedented times," another phrase that's been used umpteen million times is, "We're all in this together." Great. So what does that teach me about you?

JIM: When Budweiser created their commercial after 9/11, it wasn't a commercial about beer. It was a commercial about the grief, loss, and connection thousands of people experienced as a result. Step away from the product or service, connect with people, share concerns not promotions.

DAVE: Fast forward to Super Bowl 2021.

CAYLEN: On the eve of the COVID Superbowl, everyone was wondering—would brands try to make us smile or cry? There didn't seem to be another option.

JIM: Budweiser truly understood its target audience desperately needed a laugh in this case, looking for the light after a rotten year and moving on. How? Its ad for Bud Light Seltzer Lemonade captured the entire year playing off the simple classic dilemma, "when life gives you lemons," followed by an exaggerated depiction of lemons raining literally everywhere. Yep, that brand is "packed with lemonade flavor after a lemon of a year."

Look around at the people, companies, and industries that are having a huge impact because they're not only focused on communicating their concern, but they understand how things have shifted. They understand more people are:

- Working at home
- Connecting differently with others
- Experiencing the challenge of having adequate space to work and live
- Engaging with family, children, and homeschooling
- Worrying about their futures

- Creating new career paths

DAVE: Yessss they are, Jim. They certainly are connecting differently—on Zoom calls in a room like the one in my house with inadequate space to work, loud children and a dad worried about their future as YouTubers. But back to a serious point, you brought up 9/11. Who can forget that day? That morning a few thousand people were going about their normal work routines when, without warning, they were trapped in the towers, or on planes, suddenly making the last phone call of their lives.

CAYLEN: Like the generation before me, who knew precisely where they were and what they were doing when John F. Kennedy was assassinated, this was the dark day that would define our young lives.

DAVE: That's right, Caylen, and whether it was the Kennedy assassination or 9/11, people pulled together. But we couldn't do that when the world stopped again in 2020. The virus put up walls and pushed us physically away from each other—right when we needed that closeness. Stress hit its highest point in this country, and you could feel it anywhere you went.

Months into the pandemic, I was at the grocery store and saw an older man scream at a girl because she was going the wrong way down the one-way syrup aisle. I said to him, "They should put that reprobate in jail for her nonsense." He stared. Then smiled.

The point is that during times of high stress, we do not communicate well. Messages don't get through because minds are elsewhere.

What does get through, what connects, are the things that bring us relief from that stress. During the pandemic, when we were hearing the bad news every single day and were literally exhausted, the smallest dose of humor, be it a smile or that funny text from a friend, was so welcomed.

CAYLEN: What you're doing with that small dose of humor, Dave, is making a person walk away feeling better than before.

It's what we call micro humor. And the little moments of light can add up quickly when we are in a dark time. It's about making a person walk away feeling better than before.

That is one of the most important lessons I learned when I was attending "Hot Dog High" and training to hit the road in the Wienermobile. It wasn't always easy. There were people who wanted to come inside the giant dog for a tour when we were on our way to our next event. There were times when people were disappointed that we weren't handing out actual hot dogs. Some people wanted 30 "wiener whistles" to bring home to their grandbabies. We had to know how to lead with the positive and define the dilemma in a way that was respectful and, at the same time, left them feeling better than when they first approached us. It was a true challenge sometimes.

You go see the Wienermobile in person and then share a selfie on Instagram before even walking away because talking to those hotdoggers made you feel so darn happy. Yes, there are never-ending dilemmas today, being amplified and politicized on all channels of social media. But by approaching them with positivity and the power of an idea, perhaps you could be the shift to walking away feeling better.

JIM: One way to define the dilemma you are solving, in an intriguing way, is to let people know what's in it for them. Most people aren't used to having others put their needs first, and they'll be curious about what else you have to say.

But first *you* have to figure out what's in it for them. So, as promised a few pages back, here's my game plan for asking the right questions:

> **Don't just ask "what." Ask "why":** We've all heard the classic "Five Ws": who, what, when, where, and why. All are important, but in a business conversation, the first four just set the stage for the opportunity. Real business success is sparked by the question "why?"—which is often the *second* question asked (see the next four points!) For example: "*Why* did one product succeed while the other failed?" "*Why* has this issue surfaced again?" "*Why* do you feel that way?"

> **Don't just ask "yes or no" questions:** Unfortunately, they're often difficult to answer because of nuance. "Are

employees in your department feeling good about their jobs?" (Hmmm...well, some are, and some aren't). Instead, be more expansive; in this case, beginning with *how*: "*How* are your employees feeling about their jobs?" Then, of course, "*Why* is that?"

Don't ask leading questions. Leading questions are designed to coax someone to agree with your point of view, rather than truly listen for theirs. For example, don't ask, "How do you feel about our awesome new website?" (If I don't like it, will you be mad?) Instead, be more open: "*How* do you feel about our new website?" Then follow up with, "*Why* is that?"

Don't make assumptions: Don't assume you already know the other person's likes, dislikes, rituals, or habits, because you probably don't. A simple bad example: "When you're bored at work, do you use social media?" (Ummm...I don't get bored at work, and I don't use social media much in the first place.) Instead, this question could have been, "How are you feeling about your day at work from start to finish? Why is that, and how do you deal with it?"

Don't be judgmental: Sometimes our questions are tinged with attitude, whether we know it or not. For example, "Why is your team behind schedule?" There may be a perfectly good reason why they're behind, but the question seems accusatory. Instead, begin with an open mind:

> "How do you feel the project is going so far?" *Why* is that, and how is it going?"

CAYLEN: Once you know what's in it for them, start with the good news and the opportunity the situation poses, and then objectively define the challenge. They will not only be more apt to listen, but also to participate in finding a solution which is coming up in step number four.

TERI: Here are some real world dilemma statements from our clients:

> **Oncology Researcher:** There have been great advances in cancer but what researchers are still missing is that a cancer tumor is a system of resistance mechanisms all fighting against each other.
>
> **Dairy Farmer:** People love milk but only 2% of them will ever visit a farm. That creates mystery and fear about the way animals are treated.
>
> **Agriculture Scientist:** By the year 2050 we will need to nourish 10 billion people. That means we need to double our food supply with no increase in land.
>
> **Airline Marketing Executive:** Aviation is amazing. You can fly 600 miles an hour and end up across the world in one day. However, when you fly 400,000 passengers a day, each one of them is going to have different expectations

and concerns about their journey. How do you solve for that?

Retail CEO: Traditional advertising has been severely disrupted with billions of people around the world now owning smartphones. That means that the majority of consumers now first hear about your products socially.

Global Economist: The greatest enemy to investing is in ourselves. We all have the temptation to think short-term. Wishes and dreams can cause people to overreact, but we know that information is the greatest enemy to volatility.

Mobile Phone CEO: More than 80 million Americans experience some type of tech frustration daily. In fact, our research shows that over half of all cellphone users experience up to five tech frustrations a day.

TERI: If we listen to understand, we start to truly unveil the needs, wants, and desires of others. Everyone desires something, but often they don't feel worthy to express what that is.

JIM: Empathy is the bridge. In fact, going back to Shakespeare, most of his plays were based on the concept of empathy.

TERI: It is easier to overlook other people's problems when those problems remain hidden, alien to others.

DAVE: Finding the need behind *what you think is the need* is the way to get over that hurdle, that barrier that stands in the way of growth.

CAYLEN: You have to see things from the other person's point of view to recognize what matters most to them. Luckily with social media, we have a window to people's lives more than ever before. We can find things in common long before we even meet them in person.

TERI: As we have said, if you change the questions, by defining the unmet need, you then can change the outcomes. Empathetic communication doesn't make the problems go away but compromise, unity, and progress become much easier to reach.

STEP #4

CREATE OWNERSHIP FOR YOUR SOLUTION

Moral of the story: if people feel they are part of the answer, they will be with you, not against you in a time of change.

TERI: It is a quiet day in September in the year 1563. You down your porridge and decide you want to build a cathedral. Grabbing your sword, you head down to the mayor's straw hut to get a permit.

"Wonderful," says the mayor. "That could really boost tourism during this so-called Renaissance. How long will it take?"

"No worries," say you. "It will probably take about 150 years, meaning none of us will ever see if finished. I will need a few generations to knock this baby out. It will take about 100 million pounds of stone that all has to be hand cut using symbols from the Bible."

"Go on," said the curious mayor.

"We are not sure we can pay anyone to work on the project, but the church says we can forgive their sins," you say. "Oh, one more thing."

"Yes?" said the now enthusiastic mayor.

"Hundreds of workers will die during construction, but it is going to be one heck of a building."

Believe it or not, the cathedrals got built despite the odds. Why? When people take ownership in something, they will do anything to see it completed. Call it the art of dedication. People who worked on the cathedrals felt a higher calling. They saw the cathedral as a symbol of the solution that awaited them in the next life.

Tap into the art of dedication as you move to step number four, the solution. The answer to the unmet need you clearly defined in step number three.

CAYLEN: A solution that harkens back to your anchor statement. Something seemingly simple, but incredibly sustainable. A solution that will impact the people you have yet to serve. The science of solution combined with the dedication of the cause.

Remember my dilemma in the last chapter about people's requests during Wienermobile events and making sure we could still let them walk away happier than before? The thing about meeting hundreds of people every day is that you become really good at understanding how to manage expectations while protecting the brand at the same time. The endpoint doesn't always have to be "no." Sometimes the solution is, "how about this…" For people who wanted a tour, we'd let them poke their head inside, give them a wiener whistle and a card with the link to a virtual tour on our website. For the people who were craving a fresh hot dog, we'd give them coupons for their next hot dog purchase and offer to take their picture for social media. For the lady who wanted to fill her purse with wiener whistles for her grandbabies, we gave her one for herself for the next time she was babysitting and then thirty stickers for her to share.

By understanding the dilemma of the people you serve and reframing it in a positive way, you will please your customers 99% of the time.

TERI: My family loves to play dominoes and the dilemma we face is a never-ending argument about whether it is a game of skill or a game of luck.

DAVE: It could be a game of gravity if you stack the dominoes on their side...

JIM: Isn't that momentum, not gravity?

TERI: Whatever you call it, my point is that step number four is like dominoes of the brain. Once your brain hears and acknowledges a problem, it wants a solution.

CAYLEN: Survival instinct. Kind of like when my three-year-old hears the word "snack" and tugs on the bottom of my shirt until his belly is filled with granola bars.

TERI: And curiosity. Give me a problem and I am now curious about a solution. The two go hand in hand. Your audience is listening to you, logging your logic, and anticipating the next thing you are going to say.

DAVE: "Logging your logic." Is that a real thing? Let's find out by going back to the cathedral. The project has started. Let's listen in as construction ensues. A meeting of the cathedral authorities of Italy in the year 1418.

> **Alessio:** As you know, today's meeting is to select the architect who will design the dome for our magnificent Cathedral.
>
> **Carlo:** It's about time. They started building the Cathedral in 1293.
>
> **Alessio:** I know, I know. Today we are interviewing architect Filippo Brunelleschi.
>
> **Ottavio:** Can we call him Bruno?
>
> **Alessio:** I don't care what you call him. Just listen to ideas. Here he comes.

Brunelleschi: Members of the commission, thank you for this opportunity.

Ottavio: We've heard great things about you. Tell us, have you brought ideas on how to construct the finest dome in the world?

Brunelleschi: Indeed I have. But before I show you my plans, I want to know if any of you can balance this egg I have on the table.

Carlo: Okay, looks like it will be another hundred years.

Alessio: It's impossible.

Ottavio: Can't be done.

Brunelleschi cracks open the egg on the table and puts one half of the shell on top of the other.

Carlo: Now who's going to clean that up.

Brunelleschi: Not the point. The only way we can construct the largest dome in the world is a double shell supported by pillars. The inner will be sandstone and marble, the outer bricks and mortar.

And it was shortly thereafter that Brunelleschi began his masterpiece, now known as the Duomo of Florence. He not only came up with the first design of its kind, he had to invent the construction methods that were now required to build this dome. He even had to design the tools for the project. It is the definition of innovation and originality and is why he is regarded as the greatest architect and engineer of the Renaissance.

JIM: Again, to Teri's point, when people take ownership in something, they will do anything to see it completed. People who worked on the cathedrals felt a higher calling. They saw the cathedral as a symbol of the solution that awaited them in the next life.

CAYLEN: In other words, they were motivated to complete the cathedral because they felt they were solving an unmet need on what could happen to them after they die.

TERI: Exactly. Problem plus solution equals result.

DAVE: If your solution is going to be the foundation for a new chapter for your company or organization, then that solution has to be strong enough to withstand the test of time. Just like the cathedral.

CAYLEN: It also has to be a solution where everybody feels like they have a role to play, so they're more likely to participate in a committed, meaningful way. Again, some call it "buy-in," but "ownership" is more powerful.

TERI: When I was growing up, I saw this amazing film called *Lilies of the Field*, starring Sidney Poitier. It was a beautiful film about a group of nuns who were very determined to build a chapel in a desolate area.

When they met Sidney Portier, a local handyman, they convinced him to build the chapel. Even though there were many people in the community who wanted to come and help, he wanted to do it by himself. In fact, he insisted on doing it himself. Before long, however, it became apparent that he was making very little progress.

What he eventually came to realize is that when he let other people from town come and help him, the community effort would allow that chapel to last not for just ten years, but for hundreds of years. It had little to do with the quality of the build and more to do with the fact that, because people felt ownership in the final church that was built, they would not only bring their families for generations to come, but they would take care of it with great pride.

DAVE: The strongest cathedrals are created when everyone is a builder. Ownership matters. It's human nature to care for the things we've invested personal effort in.

JIM: It's why teenagers take such immaculate care of their very first car. It's why small, family-owned businesses tend to have very loyal customers. It is why parents involve their little ones in the kitchen so they will actually eat their vegetables.

TERI: The *Lilies of the Field* is an excellent example of how a complicated story can be simply told. That's what you want, for others to remember and continue to tell your story for you.

Why? Because if they can tell the story *for you,* they take ownership of the story and make it even more personal.

CAYLEN: Most kids have heard the story of the day they were born or adopted, from their parents over and over again.

TERI: I have five children. Dave and Jim both have four kids each and Caylen has two little boys. We know this: how a child comes into this world is a story that can always be told with great pride. And because that story can be told, it becomes a unifier for each family.

CAYLEN: What do you mean?

TERI: In tough times, what does a mother do when her teenager is up in his room crying? She goes up, sits down beside him, and says, "All will be well. Let me tell you the story of the day you were born because it was the most beautiful moment in my life." That helps the child work through strife because of the power of a simple story that can be simply told.

I bring this up here because it's so important for people to be able to share the story for you. Most parents can, at a moment's notice, tell the story of when their child joined the family, because it's a story that's been told over and over again. It has a flow and a format.

CAYLEN: So when you add your solution to the unmet need, you are building the story. That could be the story of your family, your company, or your medical discovery.

JIM: You already have the moral of your story from your anchor statement, and you have established trust, via step number two, so the narrative is now becoming real.

DAVE: Here is an example. Ancestry.com has helped millions of people trace their family tree and understand more about their relatives. Is there a market or need for that? There is.

TERI: Studies have shown that three out of four people in America today cannot identify all four of their grandparents. People don't even know where they came from beyond their current family members. They're yearning for that simple story of their origins that can be simply told. Ancestry.com satisfies that yearning. It's a modern example of a company who has helped others take ownership of story because they were able to tell their own story first.

CAYLEN: They have a solution to a human origin curiosity, an unmet need, and they position it just that way. Problem plus solution equals impact.

TERI: It is essential that you understand the unmet need first so that you are delivering the right solution to the right audience at the right time.

JIM: That is the story of creating an ad centered around a product as a solution. You do the market research first, then you bring in creative.

DAVE: That is why our method has to go in the right order.

TERI: Here are examples of other solution statements from some of our clients. Note that, like your anchor, it has to be a short, significant sentence. A bit of a disrupter. Disruption can spur growth.

> **Technology CEO:** We are taking manufacturing to a whole new level and actually expanding human possibility by combining the imagination of people with the potential of machines.
>
> **Diversity and Inclusion Leader:** People and culture are intertwined because culture is how you empower and inspire people to do things never thought possible.
>
> **Restaurant Group CEO:** People want to feel good again, and they want to start by feeling good about food.
>
> **Hospitality CEO:** In order to serve the hospitality industry, we must be the industry. We call that true hospitality.
>
> **Airline Pilot:** It takes a smart team of people and astonishing technology to create what I call the "Gee Whiz" moment of takeoff.
>
> **Genetic Counselor:** We are activating a family tree of health with genetics as the root system.
>
> **Digital Currency CEO:** We are reinventing the way people engage with money to enable them to change their financial future. We lift people up to a whole new global layer of how we transact.

DAVE: Part of your story will ideally include an element of disruption. Disruption jars your thinking, breaks the monotony, stirs your thoughts and emotions— ideally in a very positive way.

JIM: Let's face it. How often do you hear companies tout a product feature or solution that you've heard before? Even if it's a feature you want, it doesn't motivate you because it's what I call a "must have." For example, during the COVID-19 pandemic, people were driving less and expected their auto premiums to be reduced. That's why State Farm pledged it would return up to $2 billion to its auto insurance customers. That was great. But ultimately, it was essentially a "must have." We heard similar announcements from Liberty Mutual, Allstate, Farmers, and Geico.

In general, there are four kinds of promises a company can make about its offering, each leading to a specific response: "Indifferent," "Must Have," "Interesting," and "Wow." Guess which matters most? Yep: "Wow."

For example, let's say I'm shopping for a car. The dealer shows me four cars with four different points of emphasis. She tells me Car A has a special: zero down, zero payments for six months. I'm indifferent. I've been saving for the car and plan to pay cash. Next up, she shows me Car B, with its retractable sunroof. To me, that's a "must have"—most SUVs have that these days. Third, we check out Car C, which she explains has a turbo-charged, 200 horsepower engine. That's interesting, but it would be much more important to my good friend than me. I'm a pretty slow, boring driver. (My friend thinks he's Richard Petty.) Last, we round the corner and look at Car D. This one, she explains, parallel parks itself and comes with solar panels that power the car. To that, I personally say, "Wow." I hate parallel parking and love saving the planet! (And gas money, of course.)

Those, of course, would be my *personal* reactions. The key is for the car manufacturer to know how its primary audience would react, what would truly "wow" them. Something they've never seen or heard before. Something surprising. Something disruptive.

TERI: So Jim, the moral of this story is?

JIM: It's so important to dig deeply, know your audience, and then knock their socks off with your solution as the climax of your story.

CAYLEN: And when you think about how that plays out in real life, oftentimes humor can be the solution or the tipping point in the story. For example, right before COVID-19, I was in the car with my husband and two kids. As life goes with small children, we were running late for an event in the city about 45 minutes from our house. An event that required paper tickets that incidentally were still on our kitchen counter. We realized this when we were well into our journey, so tensions were high when it dawned on us that we were ticketless.

There was a buzz of stress in the car. That quiet tension where no one is talking because everyone is mad. Suddenly, out of the blue, our four-year-old (who had just learned to read) yelled out "ADULT TOY STORE?! What! That is the silliest thing I have ever heard!" Realizing we had indeed just driven past the huge adult-themed billboard on the expressway, my husband and I choked with laughter, and the tension bubble effectively burst. All it took was a moment of humor.

DAVE: Wonderful story, Caylen. It reminds me of how my wife Erica's oncologist used humor to help in our visits. One time, Erica had been experiencing many painful days, and in our appointment she went on for about ten minutes straight to the doctor about how lousy she felt. He looked at her and said, "I understand, but what about me, what about my feelings?"

We all laughed. Even though it was only for a few seconds, we needed it. The humor lifted and helped. That leads me to a critical point about humor —the science which supports it.

TERI: Follow the science.

It's a phrase we heard often during the pandemic, second only to "it's the new normal," a cliché which should forever be banned from the English language.

JIM: We usually don't hear science and humor in the same breath. One seems so serious, the other not.

DAVE: But these two do run together. In fact, there is strong scientific and medical support for the use of humor. Following that science will lead you to an understanding of why humor produces such a strong connection, which lies at the heart of communicating.

TERI: I would imagine that if you can calm fears with humor, people are going to be much more open to your solution.

DAVE: Exactly.

In fact, leading medical institutions in the world, such as The Mayo Clinic, Johns Hopkins, and Oxford University, have all concluded that humor stimulates heart muscles, lowers blood pressure, relieves pain by releasing endorphins and improves the immune system.

JIM: Improves the immune system?

DAVE: That's right, humor can strengthen your immune system and help you live longer. The COVID pandemic caused the entire world to witness how the difference between living and dying, for many, was whether they were "immunocompromised." So yes, protecting the immune system has shot up on our list of priorities.

The simplest way to explain it is that stress harms the immune system and humor works directly against the stress hormones. Let me share with you one study which you may find interesting.

CAYLEN: I am already amused listening to a lawyer quote science...

DAVE: You're right. It would probably sound more legal if I used two "hereinafters," a "whereas," and a "de minimus" to make it sound better.

The Norwegian University of Science and Technology conducted a study that tracked 54,000 people (an enormous study group) for *fifteen years* to analyze the impact that humor has on mortality.

The findings were substantial. The women with a strong sense of humor had an 83% lower risk of death from infection, the men a 74% reduced risk.

TERI: It begs the question, "What does a sense of humor have to do with fighting an infection?"

DAVE: The researchers found that a strong sense of humor could minimize the "stressors" of daily life (such as a dad trying to get his kids off the Xbox every single day of remote schooling). In other words, a strong sense of humor can allow a person to scale down the perceived importance or stress of a situation, a process called diminishment.

As a result, the sense of humor is helping to protect the immune system, and scientists concluded that the protection of the immune system through stress reduction over a period of years led to a dramatically lower risk of death from an infection.

Therefore, when we see the humor in life's most anxious moments, it's not only a way to *use* humor, but also a step toward better health.

CAYLEN: And a step toward reaching your communication goals.

JIM: When humor reduces stress, it disarms, calms conflict, lowers tension and therein promotes social interactivity, closer bonds, engagement, and the connection that is so key.

DAVE: It's a reason why researchers advising NASA on the first manned mission to Mars have pointed to humor as a vital attribute for group dynamics, collaboration, and the creative thinking necessary for these astronauts who will be isolated on an intense journey that will take seven months just to get there.

Putting the science together may be a reason why Stanford University now offers a graduate school course called *Humor, Serious Business,* noting the unique and rare advantage humor provides by bringing humanity back into business.

That is Renaissance.

CAYLEN: And life-changing connections.

TERI: Using basic human instinct as a way to position even the most revolutionary solution as something that is not only doable, but something that is absolutely essential. When you see your audience smile, you are now on the right path.

DAVE: That is right. Humor is not about telling jokes, sometimes it is just about creating a smile.

CAYLEN: I try all the time to look for these reminders of the gift of connection and what it means to truly be human. Sometimes these connections can occur in an instant, at our time of greatest need.

After my four-year-old had a minor medical procedure, I noticed a nurse was taking care of him with a beautiful blend of kindness and focus when we rejoined him in recovery.

We spent the next hour getting to know her as she connected with my son and earned his trust. Ever so gently, she got him to drink his apple juice and calm down so she could remove his IV. While her job was to care for our son medically, she knew the importance of connection as well.

JIM: What did she do to connect?

CAYLEN: From a communication standpoint, she did three things flawlessly:

> **She found a common thread and wove it throughout our interactions**. My son brought his stuffed wolf and she immediately got him to stop crying by showing him pictures

of her own dog, who was the spitting image of my son's toy. Each time she came back, she checked on "wolfie."

She used the power of non-verbals. She would occasionally catch my eye from across the room and give a little thumbs up and shrug to check in, without having to interrupt us trying to calm our son. When we were going to go through discharge details, she knew to sit down across from us, speak softly, and lean in when we asked questions.

She knew how to use the power of laughter. This nurse knew that in these stressful hours for parents, humor can be the first step in the direction of healing. After telling my son she thought the hamster in the movie he was watching was the funniest thing she has ever seen, he would smile each time the furball appeared on screen. And she knew that sharing a story about her husband trying to sneak a new TV into the cart at Costco would take our minds off of the situation, if only for a moment.

As we left the hospital, I knew I probably would never see her again. However, she made a profound impact on our experience. A situation that my son found scary was converted into memories of apple juice and Star Wars Band-Aids. All through the power of connection.

TERI: Caylen shared that story during her TEDx Talk and people were on the edge of their seats listening to her.

JIM: During tough situations we often find strengths we never knew we had.

DAVE: And even when you are still trying to find the solution, humor will make the journey that much better. You can unite everyone behind a simple truth, a new type of value, a moment of realization.

CAYLEN: Think of the solution as your value statement. Share something that will make people say: "I want it, I might invest in it, and I am willing to wait for it."

TERI: Step number four, when done right, is your growth engine. However, growth can be seen as a source for good or something to be feared. We want our children to grow healthy and strong, but we want our cancer tumors to stop growing and go away.

Every day, you are asked to define a future that people can't see and one they really don't understand. Your job is to illustrate that future with a solution, a theme, that allows people to embrace the future. Why? Because the only way to predict the future is to create it.

Think about that the next time you enter a cathedral.

STEP #5

TURN WORDS INTO ACTION WITH PROOF

Moral of the story: People make decisions based on facts that matter

TERI: Emotions drive decisions, but we rationalize those decisions with information.

Proof points, the facts, are what ultimately create behavior change and investment in your idea. It is the closing part of your narrative and the "science" of your story. If you want to create action from your words, you have to shift from credible to believable.

JIM: This may be where the phrase "you are only as good as your word" comes from. It is not just what you say, but what you did.

DAVE: We can talk all day about problems and solutions, but people decide to act when you illustrate. That is why teachers have always used a blackboard, or even a stick in the sand. When you illustrate your idea, the wheels start to click. A few sketches on a table napkin led to $1 billion in film revenues for a little company named Pixar.

TERI: Proof points are the evidence that shows, and tells, our audience the solid evidence to support your solution.

CAYLEN: This is step number five, the last step of the method. Cue the fireworks and the champagne.

JIM: It's the final exclamation point of value in your leadership platform.

CAYLEN: Proof points bring out the impact in your plan. They can be numbers, analogies, or stories. Proof points speak to potential results, and people invest based on the future, not the past.

TERI: So it could be data in terms of the increased effectiveness of what you're offering, or numbers that indicate how much more money you can get back on your investment. Possibly it's an analogy to help people understand a new immunotherapy in cancer. It could even be defining this moment in time. A tech leader standing up and saying that in her thirty years of experience she has never seen such a pivotal moment.

DAVE: Teri, I have heard you say that the best proof points are the comparisons.

TERI: Exactly. People invest based on comparisons. You see it everywhere from Walmart to the *Wall Street Journal*. From buying shampoo to buying a stock. You make a decision based on the comparison; the perceived value that has been presented to you.

JIM: Buy low, sell high.

DAVE: Unless you are buying GameStop.

CAYLEN: A shampoo with twice as much Moroccan Oil for half the price? Yes!

JIM: I used to buy shampoo. Sigh.

CAYLEN: Proof points have to be packaged in a neat, tidy, and simple way so people remember you. You want to avoid long run-on sentences.

DAVE: The number one reason people can't handle a teleprompter is because they write sentences, not phrases.

TERI: The power of comparisons goes back to how we were taught in school. Even at a young age, your teacher used the power of comparison. "Johnny has six apples; Mary has seven oranges. What happens when they put them together in the fruit basket?" Our brains are wired to love comparisons.

You learn through comparison that you can put together two things that don't seem to necessarily belong to each other. But when you do put them together, you get an even better outcome. That's how you want to package the content of what you say.

CAYLEN: People invest and make decisions based on comparisons. So if you think of comparisons ahead of time, you can not only control the communication, but you can control what people remember and actually utilize when it's time to make a decision. It will be the "sound bite" heard 'round the world.

JIM: Steve Jobs, for example, used the slogan "1,000 songs in your pocket" to introduce the original iPod. Why? He understood the connection and passion people had for their music. He didn't lead with the technology of the iPod. He led with the feeling, the wonder, and was able to put the value of the iPod into a comparative picture people would never forget.

TERI: Here are some recent examples from those we have coached:

> **Pharmacist:** In our clinical trials, patients were able to reduce symptoms and risk of hospitalization by 70% when they received our COVID therapy within the first ten days of treatment.

> **School Nutrition Director:** Only one in five kids in the United States know where their next meal is coming from. The solution is as simple as a glass of milk. A child can get

nine essential nutrients from a 25-cent glass of milk. This includes three of the four nutrients most are lacking. We know that when kids get nourishment like this, they perform better in class.

Airline Executive: Airplane engines are powerful and durable, but like your car, the engines can get dirty and become less efficient. We are putting in place an innovative new cleaning program because a clean engine can save 3.4 million gallons of fuel a year and reduce emission by 33,000 tons.

FinTech Executive: Every day we open doors to help people take on risk. I learned about the value of money when I was at a young age, riding along in my dad's taxi and helping him count the money at night. I also learned the art of the conversation because I used to turn around in the front seat to talk to the passengers in the back. Putting those two skills together gives me a way to reach people in the most relevant way possible.

Pathologist: Pathologists are the GPS of patient care. We are the doctor's doctor because all treatment options start with the diagnosis.

Dean of Engineering School: We are a source of pride at our university. Our faculty represents 15% of the total staff but our engineering school brings in 50% of the research dollars.

National Defense Consultant: Our goal is to give the warfighter the ultimate in mobility at a time when we must change our focus to the near peer threat. What used to be a typical ground war is now about engaging an enemy who might be as capable as we are. What used to be a large force-on-force battle is now an unexpected attack with simple low-tech threats like IED's.

Entomologist: It takes just one bite to get Zika, so we did a massive education campaign in Brazil. Within thirty days, millions of people were informed about the disease, how to prevent the bite, and how to protect their family.

Digital Currency CEO: We are an open, trusted money platform. We are in 184 countries, interacting with 30 currencies, 8 crypto currencies, 23 fiat currencies, and 4 precious metals.

Medical Device Engineer: Using neuromodulation, we've been able to find the algorithm that speaks the language of the nervous system. We take the language of pain and modify it with electric therapy to put that language back into a normal state. People can get relief for their pain when all else has failed, and can get back to normal activity, often without the need for pain medication.

JIM: It is easy to see that comparisons do create memorable moments.

TERI: I have seen many scientists start to take notes during a presentation when the researchers on stage talk about increasing efficacy by 76% with only a 5% increase in side effect. A comparison. The unexpected note in music, but the most important one.

JIM: Now you are speaking my language.

TERI: Let's go to the world of music in just a moment. First, consider the fact that numbers, analogy, and history change from audience to audience.

CAYLEN: The key is to connect your world to the world of your audience through customized proof points. No one should ever do the same presentation twice. You have to adjust your proof points for each group.

When I wrote my TEDx Talk, I knew that strong comparisons would be essential to connect with the audience. I told three stories. One was about my roots and where I come from. About growing up in a media family, where my dad was one of the country's toughest investigative reporters (and adding in humor mentioning that we didn't get away with much as teenagers). Then I shared an anecdote about how the opposite of community is loneliness. And that, according to a recent study in the UK, more than half of lonely people simply miss having someone to laugh with. Their research also showed that simply being together with someone is missed most of all (52%), and 46% miss having a hug. And I ended with the story of the power of communication in the most tense moments of crisis—that time my son blurted out "adult toy store" shortly after learning to read.

TERI: As she prepared, Caylen asked herself a few key questions. What kind of pictures are timely and relevant right now? Use those analogies and metaphors. What kind of business goals does your company have? Use those data points. Who is in the audience you have yet to reach? Tell their stories.

DAVE: Caylen also keeps reminding us to be visual, be concise, and be memorable. How does that apply here?

TERI: Dave, comparisons are the best way to do that. If you watch your local news, you'll see that no matter what station you're watching, they're all giving that same six-second sound bite from the mayor. And they're going to have the same eight-second sound bite from the CEO. They all use the same thing. Even though they're competing, they're using the same quote. And they always use comparisons. So speak in comparisons if you want to control what is quoted, what is tweeted, what is remembered, and ultimately what will be used to make the final "buying" decision.

CAYLEN: And to my point about customizing, they might change the quote for the early morning news because that is a different audience than at 10 pm. As a busy working mom, I am in bed well before news, weather, and sports.

JIM: Sounds like your proof points have to hit what we talked about earlier: "so what, who cares and what's in it for me?"

CAYLEN: Yes, and one of the best ways to be true to your audience is to tell stories as a proof point. A good story allows the audience to see a little bit of themselves in you.

TERI: A good story is also a comparison of sorts because there is usually a before and after. A transformative moment.

DAVE: Stories can illuminate and empower.

CAYLEN: A good blend of stories and data points can also help you reach the consumer in all the right ways.

TERI: It sounds corny, but you want to speak from the head and the heart because ultimately you are speaking to the home.

JIM: Yep, pretty corny.

CAYLEN: One of my favorite songs in *Hamilton* is "The Room Where It Happens." That is how your stories should be told. I should feel like I am there with you.

TERI: That is true for every kind of story you might share. The story of a patient. The story of an innovation breakthrough. The story of an athlete's redemption. The story of a child who is the first in their family to go to college.

Caylen: A story within your bigger story, your narrative, is very powerful. As such it has to be told in about thirty seconds. You have to tell the story of someone who proves your point or makes you smile. And the story within a story has to be put in the right place in your storytelling.

Jim: The way that story within a story has been used in *Leadership Renaissance* is very indicative of why people really appreciate stories as a way to better absorb complicated ideas, give themselves a chance to breathe, and then really start to see themselves in the concept.

Teri: Another way to simplify complicated situations is with the power of "threes." Three is the number of balance and harmony. Earth, wind, and fire. Movie trilogies. A solid barstool. When you put things into "threes," it feels good.

Dave: If someone starts with four points, I'll walk right out of the room screaming.

Caylen: I'd like to see that. Now, when you have to talk about something negative, like an accident or layoffs in your company, you want to speak in "threes" to create a sense of certainty in an uncertain time.

Teri: I have worked as a media coach on some of the most high-profile crisis situations of the past three decades. It's always hard to do. But here is what I do. I walk into the crisis center, usually a conference room, and ask my clients: "OK, what are the three things you did almost immediately?" They tell me, then I say, "Great. Now go out into that press conference and share the three things you did in the first thirty minutes of this crisis."

CAYLEN: The premise here is that actions always speak louder than just words.

You can watch the reporters think: "Ah. They are responsive. They care. They have a plan."

JIM: So "threes" are a great way to create a sense of certainty in this world we live in. In fact, I've always been struck by the way a great deal of popular music adheres to the idea of an anchor statement and the power of threes.

TERI: I like to think that putting balance and harmony into how we speak is becoming more essential. You don't want to "flood" people with your topic. You want a "river." Floods are unpredictable and dangerous. Rivers run smooth, the water runs deep, and the journey is usually delightful.

JIM: As a musician, I agree. Here's why.

First, let's look at the similarity of music to anchor statements. Popular music almost always has a "hook," the phrase or line that is repeated and simply never forgotten. Plus, it often captures the whole point of the song in a couple of words.

In the '30s, Cole Porter made sure you'd never forget that "Anything Goes." In the '60s, Lennon and McCartney wanted you to remember it takes "Eight Days a Week" (or more) to show you care. More recently, Lady Gaga emphasized her struggles with relationships in "Bad Romance." And Pharrell Williams just wants you to join him in being "Happy."

DAVE: Eight days a week. Also a comparison. You can check two of the boxes.

JIM: The songwriters thought long and hard about how to capture the meaning of each song in a brilliant, memorable phrase, or even one word. It's a lot like an elevator pitch, but much shorter.

CAYLEN: As Teri mentioned, speaking in "threes" helps establish a degree of certainty. How does it help with balance and harmony?

JIM: It's no wonder that myriad jazz, Broadway, and pop songs through the mid-20th century used what's called the AABA structure, where each "A" is a verse, and "B" is the bridge. Notice there are three "A"s? This form literally helped shape popular music.

DAVE: Cue the *Mamma Mia* soundtrack.

JIM: No, I'm *not* talking about ABBA, that wonderful Swedish pop group. It's "AABA"—songs start with two verses that establish the main idea and melody of the song. Then comes the bridge, when the songwriter switches gears to provide a new perspective on the story at hand. Then, we hear the last verse wrap things up, emotionally returning us to the first two verses.

A few classic examples of AABA over time include: "Somewhere Over the Rainbow," "Sittin' on the Dock of the Bay," "Great Balls of Fire," "From Me to You," "Close to You," and "Just the Way You Are" (Billy Joel's version).

While this structure isn't used quite as often today, it still underscores the power of using three elements to make a point. In short, thinking in threes really works—in speaking, in writing, in music, and in life. And yes, even ABBA used a hybrid AABA structure in "Dancing Queen" (three different "A" verses and the "B" bridge thrown in a couple extra times for fun).

CAYLEN: It is always hard to define why certain songs make you feel so good. Now I am starting to get it. The power of a good playlist while out on my long runs.

DAVE: The rule of threes has also long been a staple of comedy.

> *Ladies and gentlemen, we will be serving coffee, tea, and a vaccine on our flight this afternoon.*
>
> *We've embarked on an aggressive plan for our company's future. We're going to build revenues, slash expenses, and set our competitors' pants on fire.*

The first two phrases set up the pattern, and the third has the curveball that delivers the humor.

It's useful to drill down on this a bit and ask what it is about the triplet that makes us laugh, and then why does that mean anything to our communication strategy.

After the pattern is set with the first two, we have an expectation for a third item to follow that pattern. When it doesn't, it is unexpected, and thus funny.

This is the source of energy for humor. The unexpected. The more something is unexpected, the funnier the moment.

TERI: We always encourage our clients to come up with the three top strengths of their company. The three words that define their brand. The three words that define their leadership voice.

CAYLEN: The three questions everyone should be asking about their industry right now. The three benefits a new drug will bring. The three places a virtual drone would show your staff making a difference in the community right now.

JIM: And you don't have to sweat the details. Music is essentially twelve notes between any octave: twelve notes and the octave repeats. It's the same story told over and over, forever. All any musician can offer this world is how they see those twelve notes. It's the same with letters and words.

TERI: Think about it. English words are just twenty-six letters, rearranged over and over again. All any speaker can offer this world is how they see those twenty-six letters and the words they create. That's it. And that's one of The Headliners' key points: helping you find focused, authentic, unique words to get your point across fast.

DAVE: How many words are there? Some say 1,000,000. Others, around 500,000. Shakespeare used 35,000 or so. The bottom line: You have a lot to pick from.

JIM: Here are a few, classic examples of how top brands have captured their message in just a few words:

> **Think about BMW.** It's the "Ultimate Driving Machine." Three words, yet they say a lot. If you're looking for a car that truly fulfills the thrill you get from driving, this is the one. Sure, it has all the other stuff: high technology, comfortable seats, safety elements. But a BMW is for the Dale Earnhardt or Danica Patrick in you.
>
> **Think about Apple.** They "Think Different." I know, they haven't said that since 2002, but everyone knows it. And Apple still lives by it, creating simple, cutting-edge technology with clean designs and ease of use.
>
> **Think about Starbucks.** There's no slogan here, but a mission: "To inspire and nurture the human spirit—one person, one cup, and one neighborhood at a time." What might that mean? Free Wi-Fi, large tables, soothing music,

your name on the cup? Yep. In one sentence, they explain themselves.

CAYLEN: It's interesting, Jim, how important proof points are in brand strategy.

JIM: Yes. Virtually every major global brand spends a great deal of time identifying proof points, or "reasons to believe (RTBs)" as they're often called. Brand strategy statements typically start with a customer insight, followed by the benefit offered by the product or service, and then with an RTB. And why do they call it a "reason to believe"? Because as you've said, it's critical to establish credibility which then leads to believability. Customers have to truly *believe* what you say. I once heard a client say the RTB is a light in the darkness which convinces consumers to have confidence in a brand.

DAVE: Give us some art. Some examples.

JIM: QuickBooks is trusted: it has over seven million customers globally. GM embraces climate control: it promises a huge shift to electric vehicles powered by its new Ultium battery. Geico knows you're concerned about insurance expenses: in 15 minutes it can save you 15% on car insurance. And the Biltmore Hotel in Miami knows I need a break: it has the largest hotel pool on the East Coast. Whoa! Sign me up.

CAYLEN: In today's world, there's a great deal of skepticism about any marketing promise, especially for millennials like me. I can hear my friends saying: "yeah, right." And Gen Z is already rolling their eyes at a brand if they don't know how to talk to them, in the places they are talking like Reddit and TikTok. But with a simple proof point, delivered immediately, a marketer changes the dynamic.

JIM: And interestingly, solid proof points for marketers are often similar to the kinds of proof points Teri describes for *any* important communication. They can be drawn from independent scientific trials, key industry awards, unique technology features, clear statistics, credible comparisons, or simple stories.

TERI: Here in step number five, we are coming to the end of the methodology. It's where you create behavior change. Whether that change is helping people embrace a healthier change in their lifestyle, or making an investment decision, change begins with a behavior change.

CAYLEN: It could be that you are trying to get people to switch their choice of products...or their career. Or maybe it's about your efforts to get someone to come to work for your company, and not go to the competitor across the street.

DAVE: Whatever it is, communication should be aligned with a desired behavior change.

TERI: And the way you create behavior change in step number five of the methodology is that, finally at the very end of your story building, you give your listeners a kind of comparison that makes them think, "I see the value. I want that value in my life."

CAYLEN: As you can tell in how we write, we are against the overuse of exclamation points that has been spawned by texting and tweeting. However, we do like the idea of the *virtual exclamation point.*

TERI: A virtual exclamation point is a great proof point that should be expressed as a comparison. Why? Because it has the same effect, only it's done in a more mature way. It can also be closing with an amazing story.

CAYLEN: People have a tendency to get really confused when you talk about the power of storytelling. They think you just go up there onstage and you tell all these little stories. However, what really matters most is timing—where the story is told. If you tell the story in the wrong place during your presentation, you may seem to be pandering to the crowd. But if you build up to telling the story of another person, that can be very empowering.

DAVE: This is critical in your internal communication at your organization as well. If you become known as a leader who starts every meeting by telling the story about how someone in the company created success, that's going to demonstrate your servant leadership. So telling the story within the story can be about how one person in the company persevered to make a difference.

JIM: It could be a story about what happened to you that morning in your effort to try to get to work in a traffic jam. It could be the story of a customer who has been struggling for ten years but finally found the solution to their problem due to the work of your R&D team. But putting in the story within the bigger story has a tremendous amount of impact if there's context for where you're sharing that story.

TERI: And when you put a story within a story, you have to learn to tell it in 30 seconds or less. People are usually pretty disciplined in how long they take to tell a joke. This is something you can ask Dave about. But no one understands the discipline of how to tell a story within a story. If it's more than 30 seconds, you lose the impact of the moment. So in order to tell a story within a story, it has to be, "Here's the problem. Here's how this person fixed it. And here's the result of their effort."

CAYLEN: Problem + solution = results. This is the key to creating a story within a story that has great impact.

JIM: Have you ever noticed that great athletes, musicians, speakers, writers, and artists make the difficult look easy? It's been said, and rightly so, that the easier something looks, the harder and more complex it is to do. When we see a classic piece of sculpture like Michelangelo's *David*, we don't typically take the time to think about how he carefully worked on each element to achieve that remarkable finished result.

DAVE: Michelangelo completed *David* after two other artists started and stopped the project, claiming there were "too many imperfections in the marble, and those imperfections would threaten the stability of such a large piece."

TERI: Michelangelo spent two years crafting the statue. Every muscle, every turn of the wrist, every aspect of each piece led back to the theme of the whole. That's what artists do. Their proof points might be as small as a brush stroke, but those proof points add to the sustainability of the final work of art. Great artists also know about the power of visualization.

CAYLEN: Everything you do or say or show should create vivid, compelling images and scenes in the minds of your audience. You want to pull them with your story, make them participate in their minds.

If you'll indulge me in one more Wienermobile story, it serves as a perfect example of the power of an image. For the past 15 years, when the first snowfall arrives and the thermometer drops, I know it's coming. The picture. The picture that has followed me and resurfaces like a Phoenix rising through the ashes—except this time it is rising through the dirty slush of a winter long past.

It all started on a very snowy, windy day of travel behind the wheel of the Oscar Mayer Wienermobile. My "hotdogger" partner in crime, Emily, and I were cruising along the frozen highways of rural Pennsylvania. Suddenly, the weather started to really turn nasty. It was that type of snow that is so thick you can literally only see a few feet in front of you. It would have been more dangerous to stop than keep inching along the four-lane highway.

Luckily, as hotdoggers we were highly trained in the art of maneuvering our 30-foot-meat-mobile and got through the storm into bright blue skies. The roads, however, were completely snow and ice-covered. One of these ice sheets caused us to spin out. Most people on Earth have never had the experience of spinning out, while encased in a giant faux hot dog. As someone who has, I can tell you that mentally it happened in slow motion but the superior design of the Wienermobile balanced itself before we flipped. However, despite our luck in not going off a cliff or flipping over, we did get pretty solidly wedged, face first, buns up, in a ditch. We had bruised egos, but we were safe.

We welcomed a passing state trooper, who quickly helped us. And then a less welcomed visitor… a reporter from a small local paper happened to be passing by as well. It was probably the lucky break of his journalistic career —a giant hot dog on wheels stuck in the snow, in his little town. He wanted to interview us, but we were focused on working with the authorities. However, he did take a picture.

THE picture.

The story ran in the local paper and then made its way to social media, where it has lived its life ever since.

Every single year, when this picture resurfaces, people try to post it as breaking news. "Did you see what happened to the Wienermobile?!" "Wienermobile crashes!" "Time to defrost the Wienermobile!" (and everything else inappropriate or sensationalized that you might imagine.) The first year it happened, I added a little comment to the posts that this wasn't new news and yes it happened to me. By year five I was starting to get a little irritated. Year ten I had a new baby to care about, so I let the fake newsers just make their fake news. And now, in year fifteen, I don't have to go to bat for myself because so many others do it for me. As soon as I see THE image pop up in December, the comments flood in, putting the poster in their place.

The point is, images are powerful. Images are the most sustainable way to get into the minds of the people you want to influence. And it doesn't have to be a picture. It can be a verbal comparison or a numeric stat that shifts mindsets.

TERI: You do this by creating vivid scenes. Vivid scenes are what you do when you create a picture in the minds of your audience. It's similar to how a filmmaker creates a beautiful scene in a movie to create a mood and understanding.

DAVE: You don't have to be an artist, director, or filmmaker to do this effectively. One of the things we encourage people to do, especially if they work in a complex area like engineering or science, is use verbal pictures to help people understand that there's a mode of action for technology, or what the experience would be like if people come to them and do business with them.

TERI: Here's an example of that: Imagine you're going to have a skin treatment that involves the medical procedure of using a laser. You don't want to hear the doctor say, "Let me spend five minutes explaining to you how this laser works." But if the physician says, "We're going to do this treatment. It's highly effective. It's going to take about thirty seconds. It's going to feel a little bit like a sunburn. May I begin?" You're going to say, "Sure, doctor, go ahead."

CAYLEN: Because she had just explained a very complicated concept in a visual way, and because you already understand what a sunburn is, you become a much more cooperative patient because you have a reference point.

JIM: Teri, it's interesting that you mention the importance of verbal images. It's critical in all communications, but naturally my mind jumps to music. In just a few words or phrases, the world's best songwriters can draw you completely into the world they want to share.

Think about the movie *Frozen*. Even when I'm not watching it for the fiftieth time with our family, when Idina Menzel starts singing "Let It Go," I can picture the scene immediately: a beautiful moonlit night on the mountain without a soul around.

Another example? Years ago, Billy Joel captured the essence of a distraught Pennsylvania city in "Allentown" with factories closing and laid-off workers standing in unemployment lines. And Simon & Garfunkel made it abundantly clear, with a powerful verbal image, how far they'll go to help out a loved one: *"Like a bridge over troubled water, I will lay me down."*

TERI: Every good song, and every good bridge, endures because of the infrastructure that is used to create it. A simple story, or song, or rhyme that can be simply told by others. An infrastructure, a method, that is scientific.

CAYLEN: A process you can count on but infused with examples, story, humor, and music. The art.

DAVE: There is a reason we watch our favorite movies over and over again. The narrative sweeps us into the story. Together we fight a common enemy and cheer for the heroes.

TERI: And there is always a new lesson to be learned.

You know, Dave, so much of what I teach about the power of storytelling infrastructure can be credited to the late Steve Jobs. Without totally disclosing my age, I did a lot of training in Silicon Valley in the late '80s and early '90s, when everything was changing. I watched Steve Jobs when he left Apple, moved to Pixar, and eventually came back to Apple again.

CAYLEN: He had just finished making *Toy Story*. When he returned, he started to create presentations that were much more than a bunch of data-heavy slides. He decided that, like a movie, his presentations would become an experience.

DAVE: More like the magic of theater.

TERI: When you think about how he did it way back then, he did it exactly the way that we are teaching you today. He didn't show you pictures of the device; he showed you pictures of people in the world whose lives became better because of it.

CAYLEN: He spoke in comparison. He built a narrative; he built a mystery and then had the moment of reveal.

JIM: He wore his signature black turtleneck to create an image of consistent strength in an era of change.

TERI: But he also knew how to create visualization. He understood that in life, we only want the things we can see.

I remember when I was a kid, we used to get the Sears Christmas catalog in the mailbox and my brother and sister and I would go through it saying, "I want that, I want that, and I want that!" We want the things we can see. And there's so much power in visualization.

CAYLEN: The thing is, after you give a presentation, you might not ever know the full impact you had on your audience.

TERI: And in today's virtual world, that has never been more true. You may get a few emails afterwards, but sometimes it takes months or years to understand your full impact. That was certainly true with Steve Jobs and might also be true with Elon Musk.

CAYLEN: Like the Butterfly Effect, the power of one conversation can be lasting. The first time I realized this was on an overnight flight with my four siblings. Growing up, traveling as a family was a priority for my parents. After sprinting to catch our flight, we were seated together in one of those long middle rows in the back of a huge plane. As an early twenty-something, I was hoping to just close my eyes and wake up in Chicago. So when a family with three very young kids sat in the row ahead of us, I rolled my millennial eyes and braced for a long night.

But as the plane took off into the dark sky…I was proved completely wrong. These were the most polite, quiet, peaceful children. And in those few moments when they got a little antsy, their parents were the most polite, patient people. When we landed at home bleary-eyed, I saw the family from the flight at baggage claim.

Something compelled me to say something, so I walked up to the parents and told them that while I don't have kids yet, I thought they did a great job, and their kids were so well-behaved. They both kind of looked at me like I was more than just jetlagged. Fast forward almost a year later and we were giving a speech to a group of executives. Afterward, a familiar face came up to Teri and me. "I don't know if you remember me, but we were on an overnight flight last year, and you complimented my wife and I after we landed. That meant so much to us, you'll never know. I can't believe that our paths crossed again this way today..." and he went on to continue to support us as a client.

TERI: Today, we have been immersed in a forced reset, but it has made us immensely more resourceful as humans and as communicators.

JIM: The time just before the Renaissance was one of the darkest times in world history, yet out of it came the most amazing developments, inventions, and global changes in the history of mankind.

DAVE: What began as a pandemic sparked a resurgence of innovation, philosophy, and creativity that set the stage for the world of technology and wonder we know today in so many ways.

TERI: Crisis is when you find your best self. That was true in 1520 and still true in 2021 and beyond. What makes us truly human is our ability to feel, to analyze, and adapt. Great things can come out of our darkest moments. Would it surprise you to know that the very first COVID-19 vaccine in the UK was given to a man named William Shakespeare of Warwickshire? True story. Google it.

Use this moment in time to rediscover who you are as a leader. Look beyond today's results and think about the people you have yet to serve. Be a teacher and share ideas, not messages. Push yourself out of your comfort zone with the safety of our five-step method. Life truly does begin outside of your comfort zone. We invite you to have courage, be kind, and have a few laughs along the way.

CURTAIN CALL

THE TOP FIVE TOUGHEST QUESTIONS WE GET

#1 Is social media a good thing or a necessary evil in my life?

CAYLEN: Social media is an opportunity. An opportunity for leaders to meet the people they serve in a way that would not be possible physically. Many of our clients are confused about where to start and how to use it, and so, often, they just don't even attempt it.

Like any other conversation, social media is a two-way street. As a leader, there are five top benefits to properly capitalizing on today's virtual connection options.

First, social media can be a direct path to reach people you have yet to serve and change the questions they are asking. It can provide a microphone to share the success of others, which will boost the overall image of your team both internally and externally. Also, with social media you can efficiently harness and pay respect to the influencers in your world while also enabling everyday people to go out and tell your story. Finally, social media can demystify the world of your work through the power of pictures.

TERI: While many leaders have created online profiles and half-heartedly re-posted every so often, few feel confident that they are in the right place, connecting to the right people. Oftentimes they feel like they are broadcasting to an empty room.

CAYLEN: Exactly. It is important to know that each social platform provides different opportunities. However, if you are ready to invest some time and effort into your social media presence, it will lead to richer connections and a chance to enhance your thought leadership. So where *should* you invest your time? It's hard to keep up because it seems like there are new social media platforms popping up all the time, but let's look at three that have stood the test of time:

Twitter is a living newsroom. From major global events being captured in real time to small press releases about an industry announcement, people are constantly connecting over the latest headlines. The thing about using Twitter professionally is that, unless you have the time and writing skills to consistently generate tweets and respond thoughtfully to others, it is best served as an information resource. We advise most clients to follow the media outlets, individuals, competitors, groups, or subject matter experts that would give them a well-rounded view of each day's news cycle.

Facebook connects you to family and friends. It also is a place where the people you want to reach are already having conversations, most likely on your brand/company page or related industry group pages. If you are just beginning to use social media as a business growth tool, consider creating a separate personal professional page.

LinkedIn is the best way to invest a little time and cultivate the most growth. It's the first place reporters go to prep for an interview. It's where potential employees go for a sense of leadership. It's where your next influencer or partner may meet you before you even shake their hand. A strong LinkedIn profile is the ultimate growth tool.

I don't want to break the rules of three bullets, but in this visual world, we all love Instagram and TikTok. Brands know that people are seeking posts that are simple, visual, and memorable, so use these visual mediums to show, not tell, the work you are doing and the change you are making.

JIM: I would definitely categorize myself as "social media curious." So let's say I *do* want to double down on LinkedIn as my platform of choice. What's next?

CAYLEN: Let's walk through your profile as if we were sitting together. The first thing people will see is the two pictures on your page. They should both be a picture that is vibrant and relevant to the impact of your work. Your headshot should show you in the environment you work in.

The right pictures will draw the eye to the next section, "About." This is where people usually copy and paste the first sentence from their resume. We see it as a chance to teach and share your "why." Be bold. The goal here is to give a sense of what you are all about and to keep the reader engaged enough to continue scrolling. (The anchor statement you developed earlier in the book would be powerful.) For inspiration, look up Teri and me on LinkedIn and see how we designed our profiles.

TERI: Your experience section should focus on results, the things you created during each chapter of your career. A recruiter might not know what "exceeded goals and metrics" means. Real numbers, facts, and quotes from leadership show the IMPACT you made.

Leaders and recruiters aren't going to be just looking for people who know how to strategize, but for people who know how to turn a strategy into growth for their business.

CAYLEN: And don't forget about the final sections of your profile. "Recommendations" is where people you have worked with in the past can share your strengths and what it is really like to work with you. There is nothing more powerful than a third-party endorsement. Your "Interests" section showcases the groups, individuals, and companies whom you have followed on their pages. Review the logos that show up on your profile and ask yourself: do these groups represent my personal brand? Could they bridge to growth?

JIM: One thing to keep in mind, whether it's for social media or any other communication, is the importance of clearly defining your personal brand. I suggest identifying three words or phrases that truly capture it and then using those words in everything you write. For me, that would mean...

DAVE: Michigan Alum?

JIM: That's two words, Dave. Try again.

TERI: How about *optimistic?* Jim's always looking on the bright side of life, listening for the good news, finding the proverbial silver lining.

CAYLEN: I'd also say he's a *creative gift-giver*. He loves sharing his artistic endeavors with others, including singing, playing piano, acting, writing, and photography. Like the song he loves to sing to his wife. Now *that's* "Your Song."

DAVE: I had to pay to see one of his performances, so that wasn't a gift.

JIM: Ha! Thanks. And I would say my third word is *inquisitive*. I feel I've asked as many questions as any human on earth after decades of work in market research.

Why? (There I go again...) To help my clients truly understand their customers, allowing them to boost their authenticity and generate trust. That's me. What are your three?

TERI: OK, Jim, but the rest of us will keep it short! Mine are: *energetic, humanistic, purposeful.*

CAYLEN: *Authentic, strong, motivated.*

DAVE: *Entertaining. Humorous. Fun.*

TERI: I invite you to think back on how we presented our story in this book and see if we brought to life our three words. I believe your answer will be "yes." You create trust when you know who you are and how you want to present yourself, whether that is on social media or with the person you meet on an airplane.

* * *

#2 I'm not a great joke teller. How can I use humor in my communication?

TERI: This is a very common question. We always remember the speakers who made us laugh, but most people struggle to know when, and how, to use humor.

JIM: The old adage was you should always open with a joke.

DAVE: Ahhh, but that's what everyone is expecting. It is the *unexpected* which produces the greatest humor.

I once had a woman come up to me and say, "I would love to use humor more, but I'm not funny." I told her, "No, you're not, and that's why people will never like you."

No, what I actually told her is that it is not about telling jokes or "trying to be funny." The opportunities for injecting humor present themselves every single day. The material is right in front of you. You live it. It's a matter of seeing the crazy imperfections of life, the things that drive us insane, or the dumb things we do, not for what they are, but the story they can be.

CAYLEN: Remember, one of the greatest comedies in history was Seinfeld, where they used common everyday occurrences as the source and energy of humor.

TERI: The biggest challenge to using humor in the work setting is fear. Fear of breaking some rule, fear that others aren't doing it, fear that we won't be funny.

Dave: I say, put your fears aside and give your audience a chance. A chance to smile, to laugh, yes. But also a chance for them to see you as approachable, likable, and in turn, someone who they can have confidence and trust in; because that is how humor works.

Every magnetic moment of humor can pull people together. Here are a few ways to use it:

See the humor in life's anxious and imperfect moments. The customer service agent who puts you on hold for five years. The airline that cancels your flight. The eighteen-year-old who walks into you because he refuses to lift his head from the cell phone. The salesperson who screws up your order. Your kids screaming in a store. Pick the anxious moment. It doesn't matter. We live in an imperfect world where all of us make mistakes, and we don't always respond to these situations as we should.

Here's what I want you to do. When the anxious and imperfect moments hit, recognize that, in real time, and see it through a lens of being the next humorous story you will tell. Then work those stories into your next presentation or meeting and watch how many will identify with them. And find it very funny.

See humor in your own imperfections. How other people perceive and see you. Seeing the humor in your own imperfections is commonly called self-deprecating, but there are actually two kinds. The first is how other people perceive and see you. In other words, what are they saying behind your back? Maybe it's your personality, maybe you're hyper, maybe it's your expressions, mannerisms, quirky habits, what you wear, and the list goes on.

People see these things in you every single day. If you cannot figure out what they are, it's usually the ones your spouse and kids tease you about. When you tap into that, you are *saying* what others are *seeing*. That is not only an easy source of humor, but also reveals an individual who is down-to-earth and relatable.

See the humor in your own mistakes: Life's Bloopers. Everyone loves bloopers, the "outtakes reel," from television shows and movies. It's the famous stars making mistakes, just like we do, and laughing at themselves. We see the genuine person behind the character, behind the actor. All of us experience these outtakes in our lives. Share them, this second form of self-deprecating humor, and be assured that it will not only bring out a smile in others, but also let them see a truly genuine side of you.

JIM: Dave is the pro when it comes to humor. But I love using it, and when I do, I always try to quickly read the room before launching into a funny story or whatever. Usually, I feel the positive vibe and have confidence my humor will spark some delight, not to mention open the door to more conversation and trust.

TERI: I strive for a smile and then I usually get a laugh. It makes me less nervous when creating a humorous moment if I only go for a happy face, not a roar. Comedy takes guts. I also try to use funny moments about my kids, my husband, the TV reporter, or anything having to do with the stress of travel. Those are things we can all relate to.

* * *

#3 It seems like I have to be a Hollywood producer just to do a simple presentation. How should I use all these new digital platforms like Zoom?

TERI: First of all, remember that a confident teacher will only use the tools that add to teaching ability. Most teachers only need a good whiteboard, or even a cocktail napkin on an airplane flight. Secondly, digital tools done right can enhance trust. People can actually see you now, and not just hear your voice from a conference room far, far away. Let's start with technologies like Zoom and Teams.

In the new virtual workplace, your Zoom image is your new business card. It is also the source of creativity and a chance to create a distinctive tone for your leadership brand. The problem is no one has ever been taught how to do it right. Like email and PowerPoint, it all happened so fast that the training manuals never got printed.

CAYLEN: Frame your image as if you were sitting across the table from someone. Make sure your computer lens is level with your actual eyes. Be careful what you do in gallery view because we are watching you.

JIM: I always try to nod and affirm what others are saying while I am in the gallery. I also continue to look right at the lens even when just listening.

TERI: Good move. To the audience you look totally engaged. Another important concept is light. This is something I learned as an ABC News producer.

Natural light is your friend. Try to put the light in front of your face. A ring light is your next best option.

JIM: I wear glasses so I will add in light from the side to avoid reflection from my computer screen – or from a direct ring light.

CAYLEN: You also want to have an interesting background. Sitting against a wall is called the "hostage" image. Putting items behind you that are colorful gives you a chance to show your personality.

DAVE: Avoid sitting in front of a bookcase. It has been overdone and no one could possibly read that much.

TERI: When you give a speech or present in front of a crowd, you have an audience to feed off of. In virtual presentations, that mirror is gone. Your brain is now your audience, telling you how you are doing and how you should feel. Try to make your brain happy by telling more stories or sharing examples of things you have already experienced. When you share things you have actually experienced, you find more confidence and it will show on the screen.

CAYLEN: The goal is to make the people you are talking to completely forget the fact that you are virtual. If they forget you are digitally distanced, they will be more engrossed in what you have to say.

JIM: We are not fans of virtual backgrounds (where you choose a picture and are magically dropped in front of it). Virtual screens are artificial and when you move, we lose you on the edges.

TERI: Showing video during a virtual meeting is great but keep your videos to a minute or two. If you are using slides, make sure the print is large enough for people to see.

DAVE: "Camera on" is always preferred, otherwise people are wondering what you are up to behind the scenes. If you are using the chat room while giving a presentation, make sure someone else is monitoring it for you. If too many people are chatting to each other while you are talking, that means you have lost their attention.

CAYLEN: Virtual meetings should have an agenda and the host should make sure everyone is engaged and involved. Tell them when to go on mute and when to come off.

DAVE: Why is it when someone is on mute, everyone in the meeting has to yell at them, all at the same time?

TERI: The bottom line is simplicity. Only use the digital tools you are comfortable with. People should be impressed with the way you lead and motivate, not the way you can use the latest upgrade in Zoom.

* * *

#4 Does what you wear really make a difference? How can I increase my executive presence?

TERI: We now live in a world where pictures can matter as much as words. So yes, it does matter what you wear. Your deliberate choice of clothing can be a reflection of your leadership style. Consider Queen Elizabeth. Despite her conservative decorum, she is almost always seen in bright colors. Why? "If they can't see me, they won't believe me," said the Queen.

CAYLEN: Wear color, even men, because color creates a sense of happiness. While most people are told, "No, you wear a red tie and a dark suit," we don't go that route. We say, "Wear color. Let the color create the right mood and tone for your meeting."

TERI: I went to a Catholic high school where we wore a uniform every day. Once a month, we paid money to wear jeans to school.

DAVE: I never had the option of paying to not wear my uniform. It would have been nice because the uniforms were made of a cardboard polyester. My friend's shirt burst into flames during a science experiment one time.

TERI: It became clear that when we were in uniform, we paid more attention in class. I still believe that your attitude is affected by what you wear. I always recommend that a speaker dresses just one step up from the audience.

JIM: When I began my career in advertising, I'd always wear a suit and tie. And no, not because I wanted to look like the Mad Men of old, but because that was the norm. Clients expected it. My bosses expected it. My wife expected it. (Yes, dear). But over the years, as we all know, that look evolved in a very uplifting, comfortable way... encouraging people to be more authentic and engaged in a relaxed, productive community. For me, that meant a shift to nice jeans, an open-collar shirt and decent shoes. It truly made each day a bit more enjoyable. That said, when I'm on stage with The Headliners, I'm back in a sport coat and slacks (until cocktail time, that is)!

TERI: In our new virtual world, the most important part of your wardrobe will not be found in your closet. It will be found in your mirror. Smile, posture, and poise. When you smile, your whole face takes on a new persona, even if you are wearing a mask. If you are on the phone, I hear it in your voice.

CAYLEN: Sit on the edge of your seat, pull your shoulders back, and gesture. Gestures are natural and make you look open and welcoming.

TERI: Gesture also affects the tone of your voice. You can always tell when someone is leaning on the table during a conference call. Their voice is flat and monotone. During an earnings call, we can tell you are reading a script. Gestures allow you to get more inflection in your voice. Just like singing.

JIM: Part of executive presence is not just what's in your closet. It is what's in your head.

TERI: Jim, that is so true. Many leaders have asked me over the years to help them learn to relax before going on stage or doing a live media interview.

JIM: I recommend music for personal inspiration. Pick a song that helps inspire you and gets you ready to address your audience. For me, the playlist in my head includes "Fight Song," "Don't Stop Believin'," or "This is Me" from *The Greatest Showman*. I also remember when my son, Peter, always listened to a song on his headphones before the next high school wrestling match. The song? "Defying Gravity" from *Wicked* - definitely not what you'd think a high school athlete would choose, but he loved it. It inspired him, and he usually won. (Oh, he also loved "Lose Yourself," a great Eminem song about powering through. But it's on the *explicit* list, so this

Boomer father is sticking with his "Defying Gravity" example for this book).

TERI: My kids always listen to music before a big game and indeed so do most major athletes. As a marathoner, amateur of course, I know that music helps me stay in rhythm and regulates my breathing. Breathing is so important.

CAYLEN: If you focus on three breaths, right before you speak, your brain is clear and has been well-fed by a little extra oxygen.

DAVE: Well, you should always wear a smile. (That was a layup).

TERI: In summary, your smile is your logo. Your persona is your business card, and the experience you leave behind is your trademark.

* * *

#5 How do I avoid a brain freeze when I get hostile or unexpected questions?

DAVE: Oh I had many fun ones as mayor. "Why can't you fix my parking ticket?" "Why don't you get rid of that alderman with the huge head?" "Why is your staff letting that goof who lives next to me raise chickens in his yard?"

There was a woman named Eileen, mid-70's, Irish brogue, very Catholic, who said, "Mr. Heilmann, I pray for you every day."

"Thank you, Eileen," I said.

"And I have two parking tickets I'd like you to take care of," she added.

That is Chicagoland politics—you "take care of" things.

I knew there was no way I was going to fix a ticket. But it was one of those times where you get the awkward question that puts you on the spot. You know the answer, but also know that immediately shutting that person down can be received as not respecting their emotions or sincerity in asking the question.

Humor is often the best choice when that happens.

I said, "Well, I can do that for you, Eileen, but you'll likely end up in hell for it." She laughed and paid her tickets.

JIM: I can't believe you told that nice woman she'll end up in hell. Typical politician. Seriously, though, when I get those questions, I think it can help to stop, think, and take a deep breath.

TERI: Breath is a great tool. We already told you how to use it before you speak, but it is also incredibly important during a Q and A session.

Most people breathe out when they get a tough question and sometimes that becomes a sigh. This sound becomes even more noticeable if you are on the radio or during a podcast. The smarter way to handle those three anxious seconds between the Q and the A is to breathe in. This will energize your brain, eliminate filler language, and pull your shoulders back.

CAYLEN: You can also lean in just slightly as you begin to answer or take a step toward your audience if on a stage. This shows you are ready to embrace the premise.

TERI: How you begin your answer is essential. You want to always listen to understand, not listen to reload your message.

CAYLEN: One of the phrases we seek to eliminate is "that's a great question." Not every question can possibly be great.

TERI: Rather, acknowledge the emotion in the question and respect the point of view of the person asking it. "I hear anger in your voice, and I want to understand why. Perhaps I can give you three examples of what we have done to help make your job easier..."

JIM: Politicians drive me crazy when they ignore the question....

DAVE: You know those damn politicians.

JIM: So many people are taught that you should just answer the question and then bridge to what you want to say.

TERI: Almost. It is not what you want to say, but what you want to teach. The best leaders will answer the question, bridge to a teachable example, and then stop. This is bridging done right. Why? Because the power of the bridge is not how you pivot but when you get to safe ground on the other side of the bridge.

JIM: And then what happens?

TERI: The next question you get is typically about the last thing that you said. If you bridge a tough or hostile question to a teachable example or a story, the brain of the listener now has something new to replace their original emotion.

CAYLEN: It goes back to the power of pictures and the beauty of keeping things simple, memorable, and visual.

TERI: That is a great note to end with. The power of the image is directly related to the power of imagination.

I will always hold the picture in my mind of the moment I conquered my aforementioned climb to the top of Mt. Kilimanjaro.

It takes a number of days to ascend the mountain. They have a phrase: poli, poli. It means slow down which is hard for a Type A like me.

It took us five days to get to the point from which we would tackle the summit. You set out at midnight after nervously gulping down hot tea and saying prayers with your climbing mates. Every article of clothing you brought now goes on your body.

You do the summit at night while the ground is frozen. You can't see how steep the grade is, but your body knows you are going straight up. Your water in your backpack is frozen and your porter has to shove an energy bar in your mouth because you are too dazed to figure out the wrapper.

Up, up you go knowing that with every step the oxygen is getting thinner. When you are on a single-minded journey like that, you depend upon simple benchmarks and small moments of hope. We knew that if all went well, we would reach the summit just after the sun came up, so we trudged on.

Suddenly, our porter told us to stop and he came over to me and turned off my headlamp, my only source of light. I was frightened and confused until he said turn around and look over there.

In the eastern sky of Africa, there was a slim ribbon of light at the horizon. The sun was starting to rise and that meant we no longer needed our headlamps. The slim sliver of light was our message that our goal was in reach.

We could see, so we believed.

To be the most impactful leader, help people to see what's beyond fear. Help people to see what the future could be. Let your words inspire them to take action. Be a teacher, not a teller and embrace the art and the science of leadership voice.

Your own personal renaissance that DaVinci, or even perhaps young Amanda Gorman, would be proud of.

> "There is always light if only we're brave enough to see it. If only we are brave enough to be it."
>
> ***--Amanda Gorman***

THE STAGE IS NOW YOURS

TO THINE OWN SELF BE TRUE

"I hear and I forget. I see and I remember.
I do and I understand."—Confucius

We laugh every time we try to share those words of wisdom from Confucius because we usually forget exactly what he said. His point exactly. Communication, even on the best of days among the savviest of people, can be challenging. But it can also be inspiring, motivating, and transforming.

The best way to remember what you have learned in *The Leadership Renaissance* is to start using it, right now. Like a golf swing, or a good recipe, the more you use your new technique, the faster it becomes a part of you.

We suggest you create your leadership platform, the story of you, using our five-step method. You can immediately use that platform in your meetings, presentations, and in your social media presence. Many of our clients start with their LinkedIn profile, as Caylen taught us a few pages back. Another way to share *The Leadership Renaissance* with your team would be with a live performance and training session from The Headliners.

Live on stage, we will bring the five-step method to life with comedy, music, and interactive role play. We will focus on what makes your organization special and uplift the audience with content written just for them. We offer simple models that can be used every day for anything from a live media interview to email to a one-minute elevator pitch with a client. That is why our method is being used by some of the most dynamic leaders around the world. It is practical, authentic, and designed to drive results.

More specifically, The Headliners is an engaging 90-minute training experience that includes:

- An exclusive five-step communication method for personal and professional growth.

- Instruction on how to use unexpected humor as a way to connect.
- Creative ways to live your brand and accelerate leadership through the power of words.
- A character-building experience that only happens when you go outside your comfort zone.
- A clear picture of how to build and deliver the ultimate one-minute pitch.

No training is ever the same and that is how it should be because your team members are not the same. As coaches, The Headliners delight in finding strengths within you that you may not be able to see on your own. Even Tom Brady needs a coach. Check us out at www.theheadlinersinfo.com.

We are inspired by the late art historian Gustav Friedrich who once shared a wonderful piece of wisdom on how to teach in the most effective way possible. "First delight and then instruct," he said. We will make you smile while you are learning, and a smile can be the first step to a new day and a new way of thinking.

The journey is under your control. No matter where you are in life, you have the power of your own words. The power of your own unique way of presenting yourself to the world. Your own unique history and your own unique wisdom to share. It all starts with you. The art, the science, the renaissance.

We greatly value the opportunity you gave us to spend time with you while you took time to read this book. We'd like to take just a few more minutes to make a small request.

Please share the impact of what you have learned with others by sharing this book. Our intent is to stimulate better connections between all people, whether it is your neighbor or a customer in another country.

But most of all, please share what worked for you by writing a review on Amazon. A few lines would be great. We look forward to being *your* reader now and learning more about the impact this book had on you, and what you gained from reading it.

How to Leave a Review?

Go to Amazon (www.amazon.com), look up the title, ***The Leadership Renaissance: Blending the Art and Science of You in Five Simple Steps*** **By: The Headliners** and type in a short review. Even if you have only read a couple of chapters, reviews truly make a difference for readers and the authors. In our content-cluttered world, books succeed by the kind, generous time readers take to leave honest reviews. Your impressions and takeaways matter. We thank you in advance for this very kind gesture. And, finally, if you would like to reach out to us with questions or comments about the book, please feel free to email us at: info@goudiemedia.com

Keep your thoughts positive because your thoughts become your words.

Keep your words positive because your words become your behavior.

Keep your behaviors positive because your behavior becomes your habits.

Keep your habits positive because your habits become your values.

Keep your values positive because they become your destiny.

-- Mahatma Gandhi

YOUR SIMPLE RECIPE FOR SUCCESS

THE HEADLINERS 5-STEP PROCESS

Use storytelling infrastructure to put your steps into an arc full of logic and energy. This allows others to then tell the story for you. A complete story, a master narrative, makes you look at things differently than you did before.

1. **Be a teacher, not a teller**. Start with your *anchor statement* to disrupt the moment and change the questions people are asking. This is the most important idea you want to teach. Define this moment in time.

2. **Give your audience a reason to listen to you.** What do you have in common with your audience? What is the source of your information? People will trust you if they know you trust them.

3. **Use the disruptive force of unmet need**. Define the dilemma you are solving in an intriguing way. Start

with the good news, the opportunity, and then objectively define the challenge.

4. **Create ownership for your solution.** If people feel ownership for your solution, they will be with you, not against you, in a time of change.
5. **Turn words into action with proof.** Use comparative numbers, analogies, and historic references to change behaviors and spur investment for a better future.

Made in the USA
Monee, IL
15 September 2021

78121922R00098